ULTIMATE
GRAB A PENCIL®
LARGE PRINT
CROSS WORDS

RICHARD MANCHESTER

BRISTOL
PARK
BOOKS

Please visit www.pennydellpuzzles.com for more great puzzles

This Bristol Park Books edition published in 2022

Bristol Park Books
3300 Park Avenue
233
Wantagh, NY 11793
www.bristolparkbooks.net

Bristol Park Books is a registered trademark of Bristol Park Books, Inc.
Published by arrangement with Penny Press, Inc.

ISBN: 978-0-88486-786-9

Printed in the United States of America

PUZZLES

1

ACROSS

1. Companions
5. Performs onstage
9. Fashionable
12. Segment
13. Condo's kin: hyph.
14. Item chosen at random
15. Excel
16. Competent
17. Golfer's prop
18. Royal messenger
20. Computer food
22. Limerick, e.g.
24. Chain of hills
27. No longer is
30. Leave out
32. Rope
33. Under the weather
34. Longed
36. Equipment
37. Retreat
39. Certain soft drink
40. 007, e.g.
41. Watchers
43. Relaxation
45. College teacher, for short
47. Phantoms
51. Floral wreath
53. Not far off
55. Halt, to a horse
56. Have
57. Festive celebration
58. Long time periods
59. Mrs. Al Bundy
60. Part of a goblet
61. At a ___ (puzzled)

DOWN

1. Shove
2. Pot donation
3. Someone who fibs
4. Watchband
5. Educational
6. Corn piece
7. Related
8. Pickle portion
9. Bullfighters
10. Less than two
11. Colorize
19. Chicago section
21. ___-tac-toe
23. Of small importance
25. Grasp
26. Uneasy
27. Bride
28. Confederate
29. Dozing
31. Morse message
35. Punctuation mark
38. Miscalculate
42. Ballads
44. Drying cloth
46. Achievement
48. Scram!
49. Heavy weights
50. Lip
51. Crop
52. Ma that baas
54. Pub brew

2

ACROSS

1. Yellow-pages fillers
4. Casual conversation
8. Farmer's measure
12. Ordinance
13. Assistant
14. Not far off
15. Hurricane part
16. Originate
17. Actress Deborah ——
18. Night before Christmas
20. Throbs
22. Grade, as a film
24. Without others
26. Pacify
28. Scratchy
32. Admission price
33. Long pole
35. Fish eggs
36. Quality
38. Movie ad
40. Duplicate
42. No ifs, ——, or buts
43. Realm
46. Squid's fluid
47. —— tie
48. Sampling of voters
51. Not high
54. Smudge
55. Adored one
56. Corn spike
57. Does needlework
58. Young society entrants
59. Lacking water

DOWN

1. Tavern offering
2. Sunrise to sunset
3. Climbing flower: 2 wds.
4. Occurrence
5. Popular show
6. Fruity beverage
7. Beat
8. Sock type
9. Third letters
10. Not well-done
11. Sins
19. Flying formation
21. Come together
22. River craft
23. Imitator
24. Fireplace dust
25. Jumped
27. Out of bed
29. Rumpled
30. Did garden work
31. Evergreen plants
34. To's companion
37. Fools
39. Rip —— Winkle
41. Barely warm
43. Decreases
44. Birthmark
45. Till
46. Sicknesses
49. Lyric verse
50. Soft toss
52. Paddle's cousin
53. Twisted, as a grin

3

ACROSS

1. Atlantic fishes
5. Slangy film
8. Copenhagen native
12. Cookie cooker
13. 100%
14. Informed about: 2 wds.
15. Colonize again
17. Baby-sit
18. Less moist
19. Parodies
21. Seize
23. TKO caller
24. To each his ___
26. Fall bloomer, for short
28. Caregiver
32. Reporter's question
34. Dunk
36. Sideways glance
37. Harplike instruments
39. Adams of "Gunsmoke"
41. Military conflict
42. Pinch hitter
44. Pocket bread
46. Classifiers
50. Canvas covers
53. Sinister
54. Audience member
56. Decorative fabric
57. Infant's sound
58. Lady's guy
59. Ran off
60. 007, e.g.
61. Betting numbers

DOWN

1. Thin rope
2. Aloft
3. Stylist
4. Nasty smile
5. Butter serving
6. Woes
7. Unobstructed
8. Obedient
9. Imitator
10. Goose egg
11. Make ___ meet (get by)
16. London streetcar
20. Bowling frames
22. Public conveyance
24. Night bird
25. For what reason?
27. In fashion
29. Gave a bonus to
30. Black or Caspian
31. Drop the ball
33. Snuggled
35. Small explosion
38. Take legal action
40. Refer to
43. Boasts
45. Dramatic dance
46. ___-esteem
47. Egg shape
48. Food staple
49. Halt
51. Await judgment
52. Arrays
55. Yo-yo, e.g.

4

ACROSS

1. Mavens
5. Electrical unit, for short
8. Former GIs
12. Question starter
13. Feather scarf
14. Grimm villain
15. Deep affection
16. Certain youth-group member: 2 wds.
18. Add sugar to
20. Gentles
21. Manta ____
22. Maui dance
23. Title giver
26. Dinner roll
27. Not used
30. Bone-dry
31. Flight
32. Provoke
33. Author
34. Physique, for short
35. Distributed
36. Stash away
38. Attack!
39. Sacrifice table
41. Math subject
45. Dauntlessly
47. Actor Martin
48. Constant
49. Feel awful
50. Bridge hand
51. Pepper's companion
52. Hog haven
53. Deceive

DOWN

1. Pointy tools
2. Hearty meal
3. Icicle locale
4. Piloted
5. Convent
6. Lunar body
7. Income
8. Outspoken
9. "I" problem?
10. Correct
11. Congeals
17. Overwhelm
19. Gob
22. Steady drone
23. Doze
24. Common verb
25. Medieval singer
26. Evil
28. Addition
29. Moist
31. First gear
32. Shrunk
34. Hatched
35. Get
37. Pollute
38. Cunningly
39. Grape drinks
40. Volcano flow
41. Landed
42. Sweetheart
43. Grate
44. Opening wager
46. Empty talk

5

ACROSS

1. Tibetan priest
5. Mince
9. Hair preparation
12. Did well on
13. Toward
14. Crude metal
15. Burn
16. Muleheaded
18. Abominable Snowman
19. Likewise not
20. Be buoyant
24. Eons
28. Drained
31. Provide
32. Golly's partner
33. Investigate
36. Mend
37. Clutch
39. Nasty
41. Auction
42. Wary
43. Cry of delight
45. Ponder
49. Long-snouted fish: 2 wds.
54. Heehaw
55. Container
56. Anytime
57. Rude look
58. Peeved
59. Price
60. Rents out

DOWN

1. Frilly
2. Long
3. Beef
4. Aimless
5. Not hers
6. Hill builder
7. Trick
8. Wanderer
9. Sticky glop
10. Mess up
11. Cariou of "Sweeney Todd"
17. Boast
21. Mouth part
22. Above, in verse
23. Brick house
25. Talent
26. Wicked
27. Alluring
28. Omelet ingredients
29. Simple
30. Chime
34. Queen ____
35. Cauliflower ____
38. Dull
40. Sign
42. Immature insect
44. Weeder
46. Spur
47. Snow melter
48. Views
49. Quantity
50. Period of time
51. Also
52. Adjust
53. Prior to, in poetry

6

ACROSS

1. Inquires
5. Spoil
8. Martial __
12. Comedy act
13. Have bills
14. Lure
15. Flat bread
16. Zip
17. Grimm villain
18. Made holy
20. Think
21. Wandered
24. Cold cubes
26. Infernos
27. Flower
31. Certain pilot
32. Piece of paper
34. Tinge
35. Carrot-top
37. Tiny amount
39. Several
40. Purchased
41. Russian emperor
44. Spherical
46. Earsplitting
47. Creeper
48. Imprint firmly
52. Initial bet
53. Fourth letter
54. Scram!
55. Sign gas
56. Blunder
57. Classify

DOWN

1. Deadly snake
2. Slalom
3. Equipment
4. Steady
5. Powered bicycle
6. Amazes
7. Turtle, e.g.
8. Dwellings
9. Storm
10. Get sleepy
11. Goblet feature
19. Abate
21. Remotely
22. Rodents
23. Brought up
25. Natural fabric
27. Sleep locale
28. Rug variety
29. Painful comment
30. Tournament
33. Country outing
36. Solidify
38. Most impolite
40. Customer
41. Tribe
42. Sector
43. Motorcar
45. Across
49. Old pronoun
50. Police officer
51. Shed tool

7

ACROSS

1. Sleeve contents
4. Formally proper
8. Tavern orders
12. Certain legume
13. Sedan, e.g.
14. Roll of fabric
15. Shady tree
16. Meaning
17. Not pretty
18. Gift-wrapping material
20. Sizzling
22. Endured
23. Common
27. Toastier
31. Tissue layer
32. Bothers
35. Cochlea site
36. Land surrounded by water
37. Bambi's mom, e.g.
38. Carry too far
40. Make like a bloodhound
42. Scratchy
46. Had pasta
48. Sweetie
49. Circular plate
52. Taunt
54. Significant period
55. Feel a dull pain
56. Apple middle
57. Part of mpg
58. Gentle creature
59. Weeder
60. Superman's logo

DOWN

1. Imitators
2. Ignited again
3. Caribbean dance
4. Chinese temple
5. Demolish
6. Part of TGIF
7. Wool eater
8. Borders on
9. Fireplace fuel
10. House addition
11. Dirty place
19. Hair accessories
21. "___ House" (song)
24. Times of good fortune
25. Fully
26. Caustic stuff
28. Gun, as a motor
29. Ms. West
30. Botch things up
32. Subway posters
33. Electrified particle
34. Aloha gift
36. Tad
38. Frequently, to Keats
39. Weight-watcher
41. Pretender
43. Wrinkly paper
44. Takes on
45. Century units
47. Imprint firmly
48. Critical
49. Male parent
50. Decorate with frosting
51. Feminine pronoun
53. Romance

8

ACROSS

1. Singer Domino
5. Decompose
8. Couples
12. Laugh-a-minute
13. ___ out (barely make)
14. Metal bar
15. Skunk feature
16. Golf norm
17. Hideous
18. Restaurant list
19. Harplike instruments
21. "___ Freedom"
23. Separate
27. Use a pipe
30. In good shape
31. It's a ___!
32. Rowboat accessory
33. Sports facility
35. Acorn-bearing tree
36. Woodchopper's tool
37. Church seat
38. Topic
40. Showed affection to
42. Green veggie
43. Overly modest one
45. Electric lamp feature
49. Rose or Seeger
52. Bilk
53. Long
54. Chef's appliance
55. Geologic division
56. Send off
57. Circus shelter
58. Like some martinis
59. Fish catchers

DOWN

1. Out of
2. Attendant
3. "Tiny ___ Adventures"
4. Hit
5. Respond
6. Approval word
7. Land
8. Supporting beam
9. Dog's tail motion
10. Kind of paint
11. Sneaky
20. Country home
22. Harvester
24. A woodwind
25. Prowl
26. Small child
27. Saturate
28. Long skirt
29. Mineral resources
30. Small amount
34. Marked down
39. Take place
41. Used up
42. Bronze coin
44. Entryway
46. Green citrus fruit
47. Single entity
48. Attains
49. Saucepan
50. December 31, e.g.
51. Five-and-___-cent store

9

ACROSS

1. Desertlike
5. Stinging insect
9. Barrel
12. Taboo: hyph.
13. ___ saxophone
14. Ill humor
15. Bird's shelter
16. Dress-shirt fastener
17. Gentleman's title
18. Restrain with a leash
20. Lead actor
21. Check out
23. Cow crowd
24. Simple
25. Harvester
27. Hither's partner
29. Tracking device
30. Normal
34. Newcomer to society
36. Bureau
37. Ski-lift type: hyph.
40. Whip
42. Behold
43. Latest thing
44. Polar bear's place
46. In the past
47. Larry, Curly, and Moe
48. Raw metals
51. Japanese money unit
52. Direction of the sunset
53. Tropical wood
54. Clever
55. Works by Keats
56. Askew

DOWN

1. Advice-columnist Landers
2. Shad ___
3. As a substitute
4. ___ on (love excessively)
5. Clothes cleaner
6. Make different
7. Hardy
8. Pea carrier
9. Sight
10. Vocal solos
11. Absorbent fabric
19. Neither here nor ___
20. Meaning
21. Go wrong
22. Vote for
26. Father
28. Should
31. Loosen by turning
32. Playing card
33. Caustic material
35. Bellowed
36. Scarves
37. Cafeteria platters
38. Doughnut-shaped roll
39. Pain
41. Meet the day
45. Bit
47. Couple
49. Listening organ
50. Heavens

10

ACROSS

1. Devoured
4. Scorch
8. "Planet of the ___"
12. Loud noise
13. Conceal
14. Golf hazard
15. Wobbled
17. Come in last
18. Amazes
19. Ran swiftly
20. Wandered
23. Workbench jaws
24. Fatigued
25. Join in marriage
26. Mom's man
29. Individuals
30. Car coating
31. Seventh month
32. Tiny vegetable
33. Evergreen
34. Thick soup
35. Tangle
37. Stroke lightly

38. Suggestion
40. Farm storage structure
41. Word of grief
42. Waterway's channel
46. Metal corrosion
47. Garden bloomer
48. Naval response
49. Pairs
50. Conveyor ___
51. Just bought

DOWN

1. Quick to learn
2. Shoe tip
3. Ram's counterpart
4. Munched
5. Rented
6. Fruit drinks
7. Strawberry color
8. Map collection
9. Method
10. At ___! (army command)
11. Hastened

16. Legends
19. Make free of
20. On the summit of
21. Ore pit
22. Morning meal
23. Irritate
25. "___ of the Roses"
27. Porter and stout
28. Colors the hair
30. Sense of humor
31. Panel member
33. Supporting
34. Least tanned
36. Cozy abodes
37. Courteous
38. Boathouse blades
39. Chimney duct
40. Father
42. Curved bone
43. Bar
44. Needle's hole
45. Lawn droplets

11

ACROSS

1. Leading actor
5. Disagreement
9. Squad ___
12. Masking ___
13. Fuss: hyph.
14. Small number
15. Peck film, with "The"
16. Apartment sharer
18. Compass point
19. Bungle
20. Cut down
21. Gallery display
23. Superman's logo
25. Type type
29. Hen's offspring
33. Weight measure
34. Snapshot
36. Hawaiian garland
37. Distinctive manner
39. Multiplied by two
41. Sign
43. '60s do
44. Hat edge
47. Blockhead
49. Male deer
53. Able to read
55. Big rig
56. Gulped down
57. Burn soother
58. Tall shade trees
59. Garment border
60. Spaces
61. Coin taker

DOWN

1. Store aboard a vessel
2. Domestic
3. "Planet of the ___"
4. Apartment, e.g.
5. Limber up
6. Needy
7. Love deeply
8. Actor Hanks
9. Urge
10. Opening wager
11. Stalk of grass
17. Alda's TV series
22. Develop fully
24. Scrub clean
25. ___ in the bag!
26. Tyke
27. Whichever
28. Lay lawn
30. ___ at ease
31. Third letter
32. Nanny's child
35. Chewy candies
38. Sour green fruit
40. Foremen
42. Australian "bear"
44. Dull
45. "The ___ of Spring"
46. Component
48. Sitting above
50. Swiss archer
51. Bullets
52. Meaning
54. Torn cloth

12

ACROSS

1. Milky gem
5. Bodies of water
9. Hairdo
12. Concert solo
13. Bean curd
14. Crude copper
15. Mummy's place
16. Hill builders
17. Candle count
18. Byron's above
20. Chartered
22. Brightness
25. Hide
27. Knock lightly
28. Tardy
30. Understood
34. Barely make
35. Have a bawl
36. Sailor's yes
37. Actress Mae —
39. Coarse file
41. Came across
42. Over
44. Looks suggestively
46. Beginning section
49. Coloring agent
50. Caboose, e.g.
51. Farewell: hyph.
54. Stage part
58. Formerly
59. Large test
60. Notion
61. Pumpernickel
    ingredient
62. Agts.
63. Go over copy

DOWN

1. Dobbin's grain
2. Opposite of anti
3. Focus
4. Work
5. Astral body
6. Eternity
7. Behind
8. Fish delicacy
9. Male swine
10. Compel
11. Shortcoming
19. Long fish
21. Pen fluid
22. Increased in size
23. Champlain or
    Tahoe
24. Chimpanzees
25. Scarecrow
    stuffing
26. Florida island
    group
29. Cropland
    measure
31. Designate
32. Observer
33. Sprinkles
38. Gob
40. Tissue layer
43. Memo taker
45. Ghostly
46. Froster
47. Not any
48. Birch or poplar
49. Barriers
52. Chopper
53. Knock
55. "The — Couple"
56. Floral necklace
57. Snack

13

ACROSS

1. Catcher's glove
5. Command to Fido
9. Hot Springs, e.g.
12. Again
13. Had on
14. Bathroom item
15. Mimicking bird
16. Points a gun
17. Every bit
18. Suggest
20. Besides
21. Australian animal
24. Creator
25. Rustic hotel
26. Name list
30. Angler's aid
31. Standard
32. Foot digit
35. Start a new paragraph
36. Exasperate
37. Gladiator's place
40. Game-show host
42. Damp and chilly
43. Unrefined
46. "___ to a Nightingale"
47. Garble
48. ___ of passage
52. Ms. Dawber
53. Suspend
54. Target
55. Sample
56. Border
57. Ceases

DOWN

1. Naomi, to Wynonna
2. Climbing plant
3. Finger count
4. Beaten path
5. Switch
6. Labor
7. Military body
8. Certainly!
9. Flower stem
10. Heart rate
11. More competent
19. Boat basin
20. Spike of corn
21. Relations
22. Small number
23. Picnic nuisance
24. Defrosted
27. Puzzling
28. Glimpse
29. Yellowish brown
32. Muscle twitch
33. Mine material
34. ___ out (supplement)
35. Pen fluid
37. Care for an orphan
38. Plane spotter
39. Adversary
41. Unite
43. Garbed
44. Ladder part
45. Compel
47. "___ Belongs to Me"
49. Charged atom
50. Smidgen
51. Subways' cousins

14

ACROSS

1. Linger
4. Dangerous snakes
8. Information
12. Feeling awful
13. Substitute
14. Cafe sign
15. Opponent
16. Quote
17. Disagreement
18. Gentle
20. Impersonator
22. Dissimilar
24. Kooky
27. Made like a crow
30. Coffee holder
31. Geese formation
32. Public disturbance
33. Watery juice
34. Broad valley
35. Excitement
36. ___ out (overeat)
37. Greased
38. Flower site
39. Puts on notice
41. Voter sampling
43. Yearned
47. Freighter, e.g.
49. Not busy
51. Have bills
52. Animal skin
53. Watcher
54. Fountain ___
55. Votes in agreement
56. Ruby and scarlet
57. Letter before tee

DOWN

1. Hoist
2. Burn soother
3. Valley
4. Climb upward
5. Swoosh
6. Butter piece
7. Talk louder!: 2 wds.
8. Portion of medicine
9. Permission
10. Wonderland beverage
11. Hill builder
19. Musical twosome
21. Coat holder
23. Mirror reflection
25. Take out, as text
26. Act
27. Certain shellfish
28. General's helper
29. Stack of fireplace fuel
33. More foolish
34. Part of CD
36. Friend
37. River mammals
40. Irritated
42. Chooses
44. Keep the faith
45. Mas that baa
46. Bear caves
47. Health club
48. Attention-getter
50. Color fabric

15

ACROSS

1. Fine powder
5. Scientist's locale
8. Sunrise
12. Soprano's solo
13. Under the weather
14. Reed instrument
15. Lived
16. Sign of triumph
17. Soft light
18. Wrong
20. Military cafeteria
21. Naked
24. Caribbean, e.g.
26. Tease
27. Florida island
28. Meek
31. Mousse alternative
32. Increase
34. Misfortune
35. Graceful tree
36. Possess
37. Andes animal
39. Printer's fluid
40. More profound
41. Pot covers
44. Lingers
46. Movie star, perhaps
47. Fore's opposite
48. Makes a dress
52. Kennel pest
53. Rodent pest
54. Of the mouth
55. Expression
56. Desertlike
57. Not any

DOWN

1. Restaurant check
2. "We ___ the Champions"
3. Commit perjury
4. Erie and Panama
5. Furious
6. Pub brews
7. Consecrates
8. Belief
9. Skilled
10. Romances
11. Hot tip
19. ___ of honor
21. Compulsion
22. Christmastime
23. Composed
25. Shoelace hole
27. Family
28. Trade
29. Dwelling
30. Measure of time
33. Ungainly
38. School exercise
39. Koranic faith
40. Lyric
41. Pick up
42. Loafing
43. Busy person
45. Not nearby
49. Notable time
50. Strife
51. Cunning

16

ACROSS

1. One who fibs
5. Camp beds
9. Steal from
12. Choir voice
13. Domain
14. Night before a holiday
15. Guilty, e.g.
16. Skin
17. Relaxation room
18. Appraised
20. Body of water
21. Bathing-suit top
24. Throat part
26. Shoot the breeze
27. Tyke
28. Two-person fights
32. "The ___ Cometh"
34. Come to one's aid
35. Doc
36. Green vegetable
37. Sandwich meat
38. Wave of excitement
40. Yes, to Henri
41. Amend text
44. Clean of markings
46. Pistol
47. Cover
48. Got a hole in one
52. A hardwood
53. Baseball events
54. Flounder's cousin
55. Shady
56. Lower joint
57. Mummy's place

DOWN

1. Track circuit
2. Not well
3. Had pasta
4. Lion's call
5. Comic strip
6. Adjust to surroundings
7. Leans
8. Feeling low
9. Make over
10. Cake baker
11. Twist
19. Fasten
20. Additionally
21. Lip
22. Contest
23. Parodied
25. Principles
29. Mountain refrain
30. Hawaiian party
31. Trailer truck
33. Thickly padded glove
34. Fall back
36. Sea bandit
39. Show a second time
41. Self-images
42. In two parts
43. Like writing fluid
45. Compass point
47. Stir-fry vessel
49. Pigeon sound
50. Tall tree
51. Society gal

17

ACROSS

1. Defame
5. Dad's boy
8. Appealed
12. Firefighter's need
13. Woolly mother
14. Deputy
15. Still sleeping
16. Dawn moisture
17. Wide smile
18. Good guy
19. Commercials, for short
20. Fillies' fodder
21. Convent member
23. "The ___ Squad"
25. Lucky number?
28. Baked pasta dish
32. Outrage
33. Former French coin
35. Klutz
36. Movie ad
38. Take as one's own
40. "___ Now or Never"
41. Cook in a wok
42. Female voice
45. Unfavorable
47. Long time periods
51. ___ citizenship
52. Game cube
53. Golf-bag item
54. English title
55. ___ out a living
56. Granny
57. Beef fat
58. Hardened
59. Thick stuff

DOWN

1. Persian king
2. Earring's place
3. Consumer
4. Remodeled
5. Car
6. Had a debt
7. Dan Rather, e.g.
8. Chinese temple
9. Italian money, once
10. Correct a manuscript
11. Animals' lairs
22. Incompetent
24. Hollywood award
25. Slurp
26. Go astray
27. Sign of triumph
28. Ordinance
29. Hair gel
30. Catch 40 winks
31. Behind
34. Lives
37. Reddish blue
39. Coloring
41. Group of ships
42. Inserts
43. Hawaiian feast
44. Obedient
46. "Some ___ It Hot"
48. Final exam, sometimes
49. Forbidden thing: hyph.
50. Cookie type

18

ACROSS

1. Huge
4. Loony
8. Home sites
12. Keats poem
13. Stare rudely at
14. Radiate
15. Not as tough
17. Storage tower
18. Detest
19. Cup handle
20. Dance component
21. Night before Christmas
23. Orangutan, e.g.
25. Hooded reptile
28. Cold manner
32. Exist
33. Group of judges
35. Floral garland
36. Marriage
38. Thing of worth
40. Slip up
41. Rearward, on a boat
42. Pollution
45. Have
47. Laundry appliance
51. Key —— pie
52. Housecoat
54. Congregation's reply
55. Range
56. Exclamation of pleasure
57. River curve
58. Large quiz
59. Gel

DOWN

1. The two together
2. Brainchild
3. Lady's man
4. Forest female
5. Be of the same opinion
6. Dog's hounder
7. Balcony
8. Drop off
9. Fail to mention
10. Linoleum piece
11. Desist
16. Woodland creature
22. Steam
24. Rice dish
25. Crow call
26. Mining product
27. Bunk
28. Printer's need
29. Subways' cousins
30. Realize
31. Use a throne
34. Circus gymnast
37. Fable
39. Blend
41. Stakes
42. Piece of marble
43. Silent actor
44. Foretelling sign
46. Silver or glass follower
48. Paddles
49. Clarinet's kin
50. Politician Gingrich
53. Head topper

19

ACROSS

1. Animal feed
5. Lemony drink
8. Out of town
12. Hired car
13. Type of bean
14. Steak order
15. Champs
16. Decorate a cake
17. Boat personnel
18. Chartered
20. Andes pack animals
22. Billfold item
23. Rescue
24. Gift for a teacher
27. Admires
31. Great anger
32. Strength
34. Race unit
35. Desire
37. Southpaw
39. Ump's kin
40. Gender
41. Foolish
44. Feats of magic
48. Precipitation
49. Pumpernickel ingredient
51. Cleaning agent
52. Cover with gold
53. At present
54. "A Bronx ___"
55. Architectural wings
56. Offs' opposites
57. Large quantity

DOWN

1. Play the lead
2. Decorative material
3. Beasts of burden
4. Revolver
5. Stage remark
6. Sawbones
7. By an ___ (barely)
8. Game room
9. Weatherman's word
10. Realm
11. Some evergreens
19. Foes
21. Not as large
24. Become sick
25. In favor of
26. Enclosure for animals
27. Hen output
28. Santa's worker
29. Small rug
30. Secret watcher
33. "The Towering ___"
36. Crushes
38. Has being
40. Simmers
41. Compel
42. Manicurist's concern
43. Actor Smith
45. "___ Miner's Daughter"
46. Cabbagelike veggie
47. Gush out
50. Over there, poetically

20

ACROSS

1. Venomous snakes
5. Be tardy
8. Performs
12. Cranny's kin
13. "Long, Long ___"
14. Begone!
15. Curtis or Danza
16. Written request
18. Having no boundaries
20. Prison rooms
21. Yes, to Popeye
22. Cow crowd
23. Make a home run
26. Formal address
27. "___ Been Lonely Too Long"
30. Slab
31. Small lump
32. ___-friendly
33. Lamprey, e.g.
34. Track transaction
35. Alternate
36. Gawk at
38. Fleecy critter
39. Bank
41. Changed
45. Also
47. Flatfish
48. Realm
49. Above, in poems
50. Land amid water
51. Boldly forward
52. No
53. Bruce and Brenda

DOWN

1. Poker opener
2. Before long
3. Body of water
4. "To a ___" (Shelley ode)
5. Small blunder
6. Eons
7. "I ___ You Babe"
8. Fall bloomer
9. Immature
10. Hammer or drill
11. "My Three ___"
17. Froster
19. "___ of the Needle"
22. Kept secret
23. Feminine pronoun
24. Stage prompt
25. Bystander
26. Occupied a seat
28. Victory sign
29. Mess up
31. Microscopic
32. Fork, e.g.
34. Blustered
35. Be in debt
37. Wonderful
38. Grinding material
39. Openhanded blow
40. Employ
41. On a boat
42. Portion
43. French magazine
44. Below-average grades
46. Charged particle

21

ACROSS

1. Sculpture and music
5. Cup feature
8. Persian king
12. Cashmere, e.g.
13. "___ Wednesday"
14. Ashy
15. Corporate symbol
16. Know the ___ and outs
17. Again
18. Social position
20. Cultivate
22. Defy authority
24. Agent 007, e.g.
27. Madison Avenue employee
31. Garment opening
33. Earsplitting
34. Sneaky
35. Prayer concluder
36. Proclaims
38. Suggestions
39. Movie location
40. Baker's need
42. At a loss
44. Flee
49. Comedian Little
51. "The ___ Squad"
53. Milky stone
54. Canyon's answer
55. Historic period
56. Corrals
57. Ownership document
58. Lion's home
59. On the cutting ___

DOWN

1. Piercing tools
2. Carrot or beet
3. Nero's garment
4. Coin taker
5. Elevate
6. Hotel
7. Detective story
8. Cross
9. Good-looking
10. Pub beverage
11. Chop with an axe
19. Container
21. Horror-film street
23. Hobby wood
25. Urgent request
26. Cravings
27. Woeful word
28. Pharmacist's quantity
29. Facial hair
30. Cooling drink
32. Used to own
34. Cooked with vapor
37. Bread or cereal grain
38. "___ a Wonderful Life"
41. Car type
43. Having footwear on
45. Manage
46. Copied
47. Twinge
48. Differently
49. Cincinnati player
50. Slippery surface
52. Mine find

22

ACROSS

1. Fireplace residue
4. Charge
8. Bottom of a foot
12. Besides
13. Doctor's office procedure
14. Speak to God
15. Poetic form
16. Droopy
17. Gather leaves
18. Page border
20. Labored
22. Fishing
24. American bird
27. Decreases
31. Life story, for short
32. Smidgen
33. Eat late
34. Flower
37. Premature
39. Put into words
41. Taken illegally
44. Gambling hall
48. Cab
49. Rich Little, e.g.
51. Talk idly
52. Blessing response
53. Fender imperfection
54. ___ and the same
55. Lady's man
56. Formal promise
57. Beam

DOWN

1. Nature's building block
2. Baking ingredient
3. Weeder
4. Catlike
5. Chopping
6. Thrust
7. Drained
8. Small branches
9. Word-of-mouth
10. Superior or Ontario
11. Watched
19. Lassie
21. Offs' opposites
23. Andes pack animal
24. Flow back
25. Be unwell
26. Thick substance
28. 19th letter
29. Bolt's partner
30. Snoop
32. Windstorm
35. Injured-arm support
36. "___ Done Him Wrong"
37. Fireplace
38. Public notices
40. Aroma
41. For men only
42. Domestic
43. Yoke of ___
45. Dr. Frankenstein's helper
46. Grandma
47. Heed
50. Small vegetable

23

ACROSS

1. Shoo!
6. Defective
9. Play division
12. Australian marsupial
13. Deep anger
14. Messy stuff
15. Enter data
16. Background
18. Netting
20. Inserts
21. Steals from
24. Trenches
27. Paul Bunyan's tool
28. Cabinets
32. Fill again
34. Watering hole
35. Snarled
37. Heckler's cry
38. Pub mug
39. Basil or parsley, e.g.
40. iPod type
43. Hang around
45. Not repeated: hyph.
48. Baked ___
52. Had wings
53. Amazement
54. Not illuminated
55. Head signal
56. Tokyo currency
57. Score

DOWN

1. Enjoy Aspen
2. Cheat
3. Music of Ice Cube and Hammer
4. Former students, for short
5. Comrade
6. Cathedral leader
7. Rainbow's shape
8. Barely passing grade
9. Ancient
10. Strong twine
11. Child's treasures
17. Of the nose
19. Smear
21. Hamburger order
22. Farm animals
23. Waist cinch
25. Not in school
26. Frog's warty kin
28. Is unable
29. Priest's garment
30. Entry
31. Stuck-up person
33. Caravan stopover
36. Hark!
39. Laughing ___
40. Complain
41. "___ each life . . ."
42. Destitution
44. Border on
46. Hit the ___
47. Have a debt
49. Entirety
50. Naught
51. Porker's home

24

ACROSS

1. Leatherworker's tool
4. Jail chamber
8. Bullets, for short
12. Hive dweller
13. Burn-soothing leaf
14. Recompensed
15. "All About ___"
16. Type of peach
18. Oil-well rig
20. Fasteners
21. Hill-building insect
22. Salad fish
23. Cinnamon or clove
26. "I ___ You Babe"
27. Bikini part
30. Multitude
31. Emerald or garnet
32. Large family unit
33. Bodybuilder's place
34. Color
35. Mix
36. Last word in prayer
38. Miss Piggy's "me"
39. Leading man
41. Answer
45. Keepsakes
47. Compete
48. Study steadily
49. On the cutting ___
50. Expert person
51. Went in haste
52. Hoe
53. Preceded

DOWN

1. Still not up
2. "___ Only Just Begun"
3. Sly gaze
4. Dog
5. Determine in favor of
6. Security device
7. ___ the good times roll
8. Cook's attire
9. Possible to post
10. Flavoring herb
11. Certain poems
17. Border on
19. Suggestive
22. Hanks of "Philadelphia"
23. Droop
24. Force open
25. Young
26. Wow!
28. Dashed
29. Furthermore
31. Rev, as an engine
32. Buckle
34. At this location
35. Ordered around
37. Transferred
38. Road sign
39. Poisonous snakes
40. Chicken's pen
41. Carnival attraction
42. Oblong
43. Kind
44. Real-estate document
46. Of recent origin

25

ACROSS

1. Put
4. Mouse catcher
8. Bewildered
12. Important time
13. Named in a will
14. Low wail
15. Feasible
17. Mr. Lancaster
18. Not offs
19. Rebuffs
21. Express indifference
24. Green vegetables
25. Small duck
26. Scarf
30. Corn spike
31. Depart
32. Railroad unit
33. Movie opening
35. "___ Only Just Begun"
36. Brats
37. West Point student
38. Horned animals, shortly
41. Raced
42. New England coast
43. More than adequate
48. Base
49. Gambling game
50. Dove sound
51. Winter transport
52. "The Cutting ___"
53. Make a stab at

DOWN

1. Drink like a cat
2. Before now
3. Correct!
4. Object
5. Confederates, shortly
6. Be under the weather
7. Maintain
8. Sneak attack
9. Like lemon juice
10. Bring in
11. Picnic pests
16. Inner being
20. Speed
21. Stair
22. "I ___ a Symphony"
23. Scarce
24. Bartletts and Boscs
26. Relic
27. Cooled
28. Roof part
29. Bother
31. Celebrity's transport
34. Made coins
35. Scepter
37. Hiawatha's vessel
38. Guns the engine
39. Flag down
40. Florida Key, e.g.
41. Pealed
44. Bunk
45. Ham it up
46. Neither hide ___ hair
47. Squirt gun, e.g.

26

ACROSS

1. Has obligations
5. Covered
9. Part of a train
12. Harbor city
13. Present
14. "Long ___ Tomorrow"
15. Matador's foe
16. Sturdy trees
17. Auction offer
18. Advertising lights
20. Ore source
21. Cloudiest
24. Game of chance
25. "___ Miss Brooks"
26. Ran wild
28. Acquire
30. Bob or beehive, e.g.
34. Get back
36. Help
37. Not as hazardous
40. Clipped
42. Island dance
43. More exquisite
44. Consumed food
45. Created
46. Unused
50. Fish eggs
51. Orange and grape drinks
52. Dinner, e.g.
53. Highway curve
54. Annoying person
55. Goals

DOWN

1. Select
2. Seek the love of
3. Misspeak
4. Rocky
5. Electing
6. Shed style: hyph.
7. Boats like Noah's
8. ___ Moines
9. "Uncle Tom's ___"
10. Growing older
11. Western show
19. More creepy
20. Skirt length
21. Muck
22. Chafe
23. Handiwork
24. Round cap
27. Skinniest
29. District
31. ___ session
32. Game cube
33. "The ___ Couple"
35. Stage lines
37. Divvy up
38. Sedans, e.g.
39. Runs away
41. ___ the pump
43. Lighten
45. Road diagram
47. Cub Scout group
48. Chap
49. Subways' cousins

27

ACROSS

1. Sleeves' contents
5. Wild attempt
9. Road material
12. Uncluttered
13. Bucket
14. Shelley offering
15. Train schedule
17. Slender pole
18. Capture
19. ___ of the earth
21. Squiggly swimmers
24. Pollute
27. Suave
31. Happiness
32. King Kong, e.g.
33. Leather band
35. Cured salmon
36. Slant
38. Reluctant
40. Scour
42. Practice boxing
43. Tater
45. Next after eighth
49. Inquire
51. "All My Children," e.g.: 2 wds.
54. Honolulu handout
55. "Jagged ___"
56. Verbal exam
57. Farm enclosure
58. Way out
59. Arched ceiling

DOWN

1. Aardvarks' tidbits
2. Curb
3. ___ Cass
4. Audio system
5. Mountain resort
6. Running bill
7. Suffers
8. Ewe's call
9. Mexican flatbread
10. Big fuss
11. Rosy
16. Young people
20. Fall behind
22. Thin strip
23. Fathers
25. Gas used in lights
26. Printed words
27. Minute quantities
28. Saga
29. ___ rug
30. Grate
34. Liberace's instrument
37. Dine in the evening
39. Camera stand
41. Cleared tables
44. Extinct bird
46. Roman fiddler
47. London streetcar
48. Hearty
49. Heidi's mountain
50. Notice
52. Previously
53. ___ se

28

ACROSS

1. Love seat
5. Car fuel
8. Uses a couch
12. Grand
13. ___ Van Winkle
14. Burn-soothing plant
15. Powder
16. Tangy refresher
17. Bend
18. Rains ice
20. Elegant
22. More vivacious
24. Stickum
27. Glow
31. BPOE member
32. Zilch
33. ___ your request
34. False names
37. Smudge
39. Shower staple
41. Hunting hound
44. Bothers
48. Teen skin problem
49. House annex
51. Box in
52. Blacken with flame
53. Look at
54. Hearty's companion
55. Stored
56. "___ the season . . ."
57. Large quantity

DOWN

1. Passes below the horizon
2. October stone
3. Put in order
4. Receive with favor
5. Hold tightly
6. Join forces with
7. Extraordinary
8. African tour
9. Ailments
10. Foot parts
11. Alluring
19. Golf accessory
21. Dominated
23. Light bender
24. Pod content
25. "___ I Need"
26. Move downhill
28. Imitate
29. Herbal drink
30. Stray
32. Tidiest
35. Say
36. Feminine pronoun
37. Child
38. April and May
40. Loses color
41. Rear
42. Throbbing pain
43. Fastener
45. Kind of exam
46. New Haven school
47. Gush out
50. Floral garland

ACROSS

1. Trades
6. Intertwined
11. Offhand
13. Geisha's garb
14. Meeting plan
15. Alters
16. Herbal ——
17. Legendary fire-breather
19. Disguises
20. Having footwear on
24. Annual data book
27. Lemon or lime drink
28. Satellite
29. Coal weight
31. Not speedy
32. Slip up
33. Record of events
35. Clairvoyant
37. Bullwinkle's pal
38. Flowering shrub
40. Notable age
43. Emerge from sleep
46. Taken illegally
48. Most recent
49. Labeled
50. Put forth
51. Work stations

DOWN

1. Shout to a cat
2. Salary
3. Bewildered
4. Wordplay
5. Make glum
6. Celebrity's transport
7. Church responses
8. Bamboozle
9. Discontinue
10. Rules to follow
12. Cowboy's rope
13. Beer barrels
18. Spirits
19. Small bus
21. Angel's headpiece
22. Scent
23. Wet, as with morning drops
24. Iowa town
25. Folk wisdom
26. Additional amount
30. Kindest
31. Porky's abode
34. Slid smoothly
36. Yard cleaner
37. Rave's partner
39. Relish
40. Graceful trees
41. Stench
42. Ifs, ——, or buts
43. Foamy brew
44. Polish
45. Had popcorn
47. Valuable mineral

30

ACROSS

1. In the thick of
5. Colt's mom
9. Also
12. Cuckoo
13. Steam appliance
14. Seek the love of
15. Brewery beverages
16. Strews about
18. Avenue
20. "To ___ For" (Kidman film)
21. Picasso's specialty
23. Cut wood, again
27. Afternoon sleep
30. Stovetop whistler
32. Secondhand
34. Exist
35. Successes
36. Province
39. Go bad
40. Sleek fabric
41. Foot part
42. Snaky letter
44. Make it ___ (hurry)
49. Deficiency
53. Ring of light
54. ___ soup (fog)
55. Consistent
56. October's stone
57. Bible boat
58. Rose or Seeger
59. Pull sharply

DOWN

1. Woeful exclamation
2. Shed feathers
3. Froster
4. Potion portion
5. Abuse
6. Curve
7. "___ House"
8. All
9. Overpowering respect
10. Neither's mate
11. Two, to Miguel
17. Fangs
19. Consume
22. Fortune-teller's card
24. Excite
25. Choir member
26. "The ___ Wing"
27. Macadamia, pecan, etc.
28. Adrift
29. Cheeky
31. Fuel
33. Less moist
37. Foot part
38. Tokyo currency
43. Conserve
45. Sailor's greeting
46. Mama's man
47. Agenda
48. Egg center
49. Resort hotel
50. Pronoun
51. A hardwood
52. Acquire

31

ACROSS

1. Humdinger
5. Charge
8. Camera part
12. Unseal
13. Experiment site
14. On the briny
15. James ___ (Agent 007)
16. Fireproof material
18. Competitor
20. Leaf ribs
21. Moose's relative
22. Salon treatment
23. Reverend Jackson
26. Amusing
27. Circle section
30. Positive votes
31. Tuck's partner
32. Leading lady or man
33. All ___ (wrong)
34. 2,000 pounds
35. Foe
36. Impact sound
38. Wow!
39. Punctuation mark
41. Difficulty
45. Ran
47. Crowd's sound
48. Golfers' goals
49. Former
50. Fix copy
51. If not
52. Tissue layer
53. Fox shelters

DOWN

1. Ear part
2. Once ___ a time . . .
3. Ash Wednesday's season
4. Disrobe
5. Side
6. Not west
7. Subside
8. Type of beam
9. Predict
10. Broadway sign
11. Lip
17. Fair
19. Beer's kin
22. Baby dog
23. Chat
24. Needle hole
25. Pioneers
26. Flipper
28. Male bighorn
29. Wail
31. Affirmative gesture
32. Smirked scornfully
34. Canned fish
35. Elongated fish
37. Cowboy's transportation
38. Lightheaded
39. Deal (with)
40. Milky stone
41. Hollow
42. Manner
43. Chief
44. Handicrafts
46. Whirling toy

32

ACROSS

1. Long quarrels
6. Peep
11. Darts
13. Powerful speaker
14. French dance
15. Brawn
16. Snake shape
17. Shipboard buddies
19. In the know
20. Run at full speed
21. Wandered
24. Lubricate
27. Absent
28. Faded
30. Polynesian dance
31. Santa's gift
32. Enthusiastically
34. Reduce
36. Move from side to side
39. Restless
40. Remit funds
43. On a ship
45. Break free
47. Trousers
48. Become darker
49. Hides
50. Brings up

DOWN

1. "___ the Nation"
2. Historical periods
3. Coffee containers
4. Sleepy's roommate
5. Boggy
6. Bread part
7. Contains
8. "The Seven Year ___"
9. Stage part
10. Get ready
12. Captured
13. Peck film, with "The"
18. Neatest
20. Verbalize
21. Occupied a seat
22. A couple
23. Beam
24. ___ Father (Lord's Prayer)
25. Under the weather
26. Reclined
29. Assembled
30. Coop female
33. Old Faithful, e.g.
34. Songbirds
35. Winds up
36. Yellow jacket
37. Talented
38. Soccer score
40. Dad
41. Imitator
42. Hankerings
44. "Sister ___"
46. So-so grade

33

ACROSS

1. Crow's call
4. School subject
8. Classroom furniture
12. Miner's goal
13. Drifting
14. Back then
15. Extend
17. Hang around
18. Info
19. Football player
20. Blunders
21. Wordplay
23. —— one's time
25. Compare
28. Pile
29. Era
32. Air hero
33. Picture
35. Also
36. —— your request
37. Price mark
38. Fiery crime
40. Cafe sign
42. Slick
43. Flat-topped hill
45. Broom's relative
47. Shade trees
51. Always
52. Scrape
54. Chablis, e.g.
55. Ownership paper
56. Golf teacher
57. Dog-team's vehicle
58. Observed
59. Embroider

DOWN

1. Chilled
2. Field of study
3. Departed
4. Porch welcomer
5. Pale
6. MTV viewer
7. Purse
8. Medicated
9. Pleads
10. Cut remnant
11. Florida island group
16. Show astonishment
22. Bond
24. Perfect
25. Racetrack circuit
26. Drink cubes
27. Coal oil
28. Shake
30. Thick and sticky substance
31. Vast span
34. Artificial: hyph.
39. Deli breads
41. Whittled
42. Fling
43. Kittens' sounds
44. Cruel
46. Command to a child
48. Kissing organs
49. Greater amount
50. Blizzard stuff
53. Calculate

34

ACROSS

1. Enemy
4. Voter sampling
8. Pimples
12. Say further
13. Opera solo
14. Speak to God
15. Toothed wheel
16. Citrus fruit
18. Bridge support
20. Passport endorsements
21. "___ So Shy"
22. Beatles movie
23. Confronted
26. Bear's hideout
27. Electrified atom
30. Stretched the truth
31. Strong desire
32. Predinner reading
33. Coffee server
34. Third letter
35. Parisian cap
36. "I ___ the Sheriff"
38. Succeed
39. Reporter's tidbit
41. Marvels
45. Worm-getter: 2 wds.
47. Feel ill
48. Mimicked
49. Or ___ (threat)
50. Mountain resort
51. Communists
52. Clothing colorer
53. Certain evergreen

DOWN

1. Reality
2. Bloodhound's clue
3. On ___ (tense)
4. Tapped
5. Verbal exams
6. Wire
7. Fall back
8. March's follower
9. More crunchy
10. Grandma
11. Potato buds
17. Fifty-fifty
19. Tool housing
22. Fowl
23. Winter ill
24. ___ conditioning
25. Inhibited
26. Barely passing grade
28. Individual
29. Bolt's mate
31. As of this time
32. Rectify
34. Imitation
35. Notebook
37. Contains
38. ___ for wear
39. Dry up
40. Batman's wrap
41. Tricky
42. "___ Money"
43. Fully mature
44. Deli side order
46. Sleeping spot

35

ACROSS

1. Enemies
5. Out of operation
8. Agreement
12. Out of service
13. Passing through
14. Resounding sound
15. Was a sports official
17. Mr. Cain
18. Switch options
19. Struggles for breath
20. Specter
24. Turnpike charge
26. Jerk
27. Hand gesture
28. What bit Cleopatra
31. Stubborn
33. Spookier
35. On the ___ (secretly)
36. Weeder
38. Stake
39. Avenue
40. Restless
41. Manly
44. Lodging place
46. Pale
47. Complying with authority
52. Vein, as of coal
53. Pub brew
54. False's opposite
55. Hound's quarry
56. Strawberry color
57. Of sound mind

DOWN

1. Kind of evergreen
2. Work by Keats
3. Gnome
4. Look
5. Chef's appliance
6. Celebration
7. Current fashion
8. Bicycle feature
9. Top cards
10. Guy
11. Shipping weights
16. Go bad
19. Gaiety
20. Sports sites
21. Lug
22. "___ the Lonely"
23. Go down the slopes
25. ___ the hill
27. Halt, to a horse
28. "___ Misbehavin'"
29. Groups
30. Hunter's quarry
32. Send away
34. Dripped
37. Fit for food
39. Verse
40. As well
41. Crush
42. Confused
43. Blacken
45. Must-have
47. Boat rower
48. "___ My Party"
49. Distinct period
50. "The Flying ___"
51. Crossed letter

36

ACROSS

1. Children
5. Not quite closed
9. Into thin ___
12. Slender woodwind
13. Imitation
14. Woman's undergarment
15. Give (out)
16. Full-grown
17. Command to Fido
18. Maiden
19. Eat elegantly
20. Apply
21. Wiped clean
23. Loves
26. Lag behind
27. Gatherings
28. Betrayal
30. Buddy
32. Remove from print
35. Curbed
36. Most senior
38. Current measure, for short
39. Formerly
41. Enjoyed a sandwich
42. Crack
43. Birch or oak
44. A long time
45. Pipe joint
46. Totally confused
47. Fat
48. Low grade
49. Gull-like bird
50. Clothing edges

DOWN

1. Hunter's shelter
2. On the ship
3. 100 pennies
4. Comprehend
5. Pungent
6. Connect
7. Emerges
8. Bar staple
9. Ridiculous
10. Showy blooms
11. Appraises
19. Unit of heat
22. Soft fabric
24. Draw idly
25. Possessed
27. Bad guy
29. Sign, as a check
30. Woman
31. Wavelet
33. Association
34. Honor
35. Blew up
36. Atlantic or Arctic
37. Tries out
40. ___-do-well
43. Tit for ___
44. Charcoal residue

37

ACROSS

1. Urge
5. First-aid ___
8. Snare
12. ___ out (demolish)
13. Hole in one
14. Good guy
15. On the crest
16. Definitely!
17. Foray
18. Horse's pride
19. Comic actor Carney
20. Chances
21. Bible boat
23. Des Moines locale
25. View
28. Winter ailment
29. Bikini piece
32. "You ___ Sixteen"
33. Makes a mule sound
35. Boy
36. Boxing count
37. Law student's exam
38. Current style
40. Cut to size
42. Speck of residue
43. ___ market
45. Buddy
47. Pull sharply
51. Bond
52. Quick to learn
53. Aspen, e.g.
54. "___ in a Lifetime"
55. ___ whiz!
56. Multitude
57. Garden intruder
58. Be in the wrong
59. Retail establishment

DOWN

1. Did the backstroke
2. Flat bread
3. "Wish ___ a Star"
4. Do again
5. Canoe's kin
6. Frosting user
7. Grumpily
8. Toss
9. Easy to peruse
10. Like the Sahara
11. Seed vessels
22. Jewish cleric
24. Deposes
25. Large container
26. Fierce anger
27. Paragraph part
28. Few and ___ between
30. Operated
31. Total up
34. Stampede
39. Musical beat
41. Gathered leaves
42. Modify
43. Ebb and ___
44. Joke's punch ___
46. Impersonator
48. District
49. At hand
50. Retained

38

ACROSS

1. Garden flower
5. Egyptian snake
8. Con game
12. Qualified
13. Celeb's resort
14. Flag site
15. James Brown's music
16. Nutritious bean
17. Walk aimlessly
18. Sweat
20. Moreover
21. Off course
23. Animal-exhibit park
26. Boar's home
27. Action words
31. Mature people
33. Breakfast flakes
34. Fonda or Jennings
35. Cargo weight
36. Cook in lard
37. Doing an office chore
39. Skidded
42. Forefather
47. Daft
48. Hire
49. Minimum ___
50. Again
51. Bering, e.g.
52. Land parcel
53. Coastal bird
54. Addition shape
55. Yuletide

DOWN

1. Rough file
2. Clarinet's relative
3. Speak indistinctly
4. Electric swimmers
5. Helps
6. Flashy
7. Bill settler
8. Misting device
9. "___ Hand Luke"
10. Cry of woe
11. Business note
19. Sweet roll
22. Retaliate for
23. Jolt suddenly
24. "___ to the West Wind"
25. Away
28. Ump's cousin
29. Grill's go-with
30. Crafty
32. Disappoint: 2 wds.
33. Hide
35. Christmas tree decoration
38. Interruption
39. Narrow strip
40. Solo
41. Cake froster
43. Graceful waterfowl
44. Mexican food item
45. Folklore giant
46. Film unit

39

ACROSS

1. Woeful word
5. Negative connector
8. Lads
12. Buffalo ——
13. Chimpanzee, e.g.
14. Brainchild
15. Makes bigger
17. Relish
18. Goddess, e.g.
19. Grandma
21. Eccentric person
23. Pregame period
27. Fitness place
29. Brother's sib
31. Ocean water
32. Diner sign
34. —— close for comfort
36. Conclusions
37. Bakery feature
39. No longer is
41. Field bed
42. Walk leisurely
44. Show anger
46. Told untruths
48. Period's partner
51. Cast off, as skin
54. Twice nine
56. Bait
57. Weep
58. Tortoise's competitor
59. Decade unit
60. Skirt bottom
61. Beef dish

DOWN

1. Still sleeping
2. Toe the ——
3. Crocodile's relative
4. Clean ——
5. Bug
6. Ready for business
7. Cut wood, again
8. Weird
9. Shelley offering
10. Sure!
11. Grabbed a chair
16. Bread and whiskey
20. Capture
22. Equipment
24. Pie filling
25. Destroy
26. Annoying person
27. There are seven of them
28. Segment
30. Miss Piggy, e.g.
33. Burn
35. Clod
38. Ring legend
40. Similar
43. Parasite
45. Butterflies' cousins
47. Terrible
49. Scant
50. Over
51. Stallone, to chums
52. Color shade
53. Memorable time
55. Fitness center

40

ACROSS

1. Gifted
5. Poor-box donations
9. This lady
12. Raise
13. Rich earth
14. Finger number
15. "Auntie ___"
16. Absent
17. Auction purchase
18. Till bill
19. Black-and-white animal
20. Duffer's dream
21. Washing machine cycle
23. Not by injection
25. Infinite
28. Conveyed
29. Picture mentally
31. Bull ___

33. Synagogue candelabrum
36. Remove from print
38. Razor sharpener
40. Geological period
41. Customary practice
44. Needlefish
45. Chalice
46. Durango dish
47. Ancient harp
48. Stubborn beast
49. Gumbo must
50. Additional
51. Retainer
52. Oboe insert
53. Numerical ending

DOWN

1. Suit of mail
2. Freshman's hat
3. Mourn
4. Sooner than, to Keats
5. Pond organism

6. Crazy bird?
7. Lutelike instrument
8. Besmirch
9. Dietary mainstay
10. Messenger
11. Vestibule
19. Beautician's offering
22. Type of net
24. "Submarine ___"
26. Person dubbed after another
27. 39, to Jack Benny
30. Scent organ
31. Survey
32. Pass, as hours
34. Sock pattern
35. Husky
36. Coffee choice
37. Instruct
39. Trim with a beak
42. Pasture measure
43. Incite
47. Permit

41

ACROSS

1. Skirt type
5. Drenches
9. Pump purchase
12. Valuable rocks
13. Tightly drawn
14. Ref's cousin
15. Depressions
16. Beg
17. Follower of neither
18. Resulted
20. Careless
22. Run, as a motor
23. Manufacture money
25. Had a pizza
27. Cake decorator
29. Interrupt
33. Shad ___
34. Waits in hiding
36. Feel poorly
37. Popular soda
39. Agenda
40. Foxy
41. Part of a rifle
43. Statute
45. Spread out
48. Gave consent
51. Billfold item
52. Matinee star
55. Yonder
56. Not at work
57. Oceanic movement
58. Ponder
59. Tofu bean
60. Boundaries
61. Large quantity

DOWN

1. Beauty spot
2. Hard metal
3. Old-movie feature
4. Edition
5. Wall component
6. Rowboat item
7. Flat-faced dog
8. Harsh
9. Pistols
10. Berserk
11. Agile
19. Sermon topic
21. ___ in the bag!
23. Kind of Scout badge
24. Angers
25. Circle part
26. In addition
28. Faction
30. Classy
31. Furnace fuel
32. Layer
35. Buck
38. Rail-splitter Lincoln
42. Merge
44. Stuffs
45. Dates
46. Data
47. Disobey
48. Malt beverages
49. Life of Riley
50. Depicted
53. Commotion
54. Out of the ordinary

42

ACROSS

1. Bonfire residue
4. Click
8. Fox's dance?
12. Hawaiian keepsake
13. Bagel feature
14. Drifter
15. Abated
17. Matinee hero
18. Newspaper section
19. Gave consent
21. Chanted
24. Bridge charges
26. Tarzan's chum
27. Actor Costello
28. Playful animal
32. Mushy stuff
33. More prone
35. Paul Bunyan's tool
36. Bother
38. Withered
39. Young goat
40. Type of tea
42. Understands
43. Rule
46. Weep
48. Press
49. Predict
54. Entrance barrier
55. Adds to
56. Immediately
57. Toboggan
58. ___ dish
59. Cloth coloring

DOWN

1. 100 percent
2. Witness
3. Towel word
4. Molt
5. Without pause
6. Brewery order
7. Bike part
8. Crave water
9. Went by taxi
10. Woodwind instrument
11. Related
16. Hang down
20. Fame
21. Lengthy tale
22. At the top
23. Gas used in lights
25. Exceed
27. ___ cake
29. Grab
30. Door sign
31. Scarlet, crimson, etc.
34. Built
37. Unlocked
41. Leg hinges
42. Sports facility
43. Brief jobs
44. Exam type
45. Ballot
47. Climb
50. Go down the slope
51. "War ___ Peace"
52. Nursery item
53. Ram's counterpart

43

ACROSS

1. Skilled cook
5. Make a choice
8. Certain spice
12. Center of activity
13. Beam
14. Milky gemstone
15. Territory
16. Tick off
17. School session
18. Wallet items
19. Excellent
21. Huey, Dewey, and Louie
23. Nearby
27. Santa's helper
30. Colony insect
31. Charter
32. Promote
34. Road curves
35. Charred
36. Crafty
38. Contains
39. Pilfer
40. Assigned job
42. Singer Como
44. Yup's opposite
48. Thin bit of smoke
51. Target
52. Yield to commands
53. Tooth ailment
54. Recreation spot
55. Became frayed
56. Changed the color of
57. Barnyard female
58. Butterfly snares

DOWN

1. Informal talk
2. Take on
3. Smooth
4. Smorgasbord
5. Beginning
6. Tropical bird
7. Tot
8. Slogans
9. Mock
10. Limo, e.g.
11. Popular street name
20. Paths between buildings
22. Noisemaker
24. Money
25. Adrift
26. Minus
27. Diminishes
28. Oaf
29. Links cry
33. Broke sharply
36. Line
37. Nonprofessional
41. Recognized
43. Allergic reaction
45. Certain woodwind
46. Cheeky
47. "Can't Take My ___ Off You"
48. Small lump
49. Frosty
50. That girl

44

ACROSS

1. Border on
5. Inquire
8. Fruit drinks
12. Heart
13. A mother's boy
14. Make well
15. Roman garment
16. "A Boy Named ___"
17. Passion
18. Part of a stairway
19. Clean, as a blackboard
21. Select
23. Deprive of weapons
27. Jay Silverheels role
30. ___ whillikers!
31. Besides
32. Gibbon or gorilla
33. Heavy burdens
35. Not even
36. Limousine, e.g.
37. Frosty
38. Conical abode
40. Most aged
42. Flock leader
43. Allowance
45. Grouch
49. Toothed tools
52. Limo fuel
53. Lessen
54. Inkling
55. Unprocessed metal
56. Mr. Knievel
57. Physique
58. Born
59. Bargain

DOWN

1. Deeds
2. Dismiss
3. Desire
4. Brewing vessel
5. Good quality
6. Rotten
7. Massaged
8. Pains
9. Payable now
10. Age of note
11. Prepared
20. Midday snooze
22. Shine
24. At the peak
25. Galloped
26. Pie a la ___
27. Mexican food
28. Whitish gem
29. Dull person
30. Cheery
34. Eight-sided figure
39. Hosted
41. Short paper
42. View again
44. Hard to find
46. Babble
47. On a cruise
48. Chime
49. Bro or sis
50. Big fuss
51. Got hitched

45

ACROSS

1. Broad-antlered beast
4. Flutter
8. Members-only group
12. Neptune's reign
13. Per
14. Fabled loser
15. Preacher's subject
16. Observer
17. Teenage problem
18. Acquired
20. Think constantly about
22. Deli side order
24. Saunter
26. Windstorm
28. Boxing site
32. In history
33. Lounged
35. Daddy's boy
36. Housetops
38. Cautioned
40. Worry
42. Is ill
43. Hinted
46. Sports facility
47. Lounge
48. Slender woodwind
51. Inclined
54. Shade source
55. Walk aimlessly
56. Brewed beverage
57. Foretelling sign
58. Has for dinner
59. Omelet need

DOWN

1. Hook shape
2. Floral necklace
3. Jumping Australian animal
4. A yard has three
5. Set down
6. ___ cream
7. Beat
8. Follower
9. Bridal-gown trim
10. Large vases
11. Honey makers
19. Have title to
21. Sword part
22. Constellation member
23. Trademark
24. Calculate, in a way
25. Wisdom tooth
27. Row
29. Gauge
30. Playwright Coward
31. No ifs, ___, or buts
34. Popular street
37. Dishonored
39. Sunbeam
41. Dote on
43. Choir member
44. Average
45. Happiness
46. Prized items
49. Feathery scarf
50. Certain grain
52. Wooden nail
53. "Catch me" game

46

ACROSS

1. Sin
4. Absent
8. Kickers' stands
12. By way of
13. Morse ____
14. Spindle
15. Monarchs
17. Ocean motion
18. Skirt length
19. Relieved
20. Made a choice
23. Take wing
25. Strive
26. Colorful sign
27. Filthy places
29. Summer shoe
31. Showy flower
35. Detest
37. Honey factory
38. Smidgen
41. Momma sheep
42. Adult females
43. Capsize
45. Scat!
47. ____ tie
48. Bald
52. Garfunkel et al.
53. Woes
54. Mouth feature
55. Don't leave!
56. Animal skin
57. Saute

DOWN

1. December 31, e.g.
2. Basketball hoop
3. Sharp knock
4. Pungent
5. Furniture material
6. Floating
7. Naturally!
8. So long!: 2 wds.
9. Be
10. Deacon
11. Shabby
16. Alters
19. Observer
20. Offs' opposites
21. Green vegetable
22. Coal weight
24. Big cat
27. Not speedy
28. Yale, e.g.
30. Scored highly
32. That fellow
33. First-person contraction
34. Burrow
36. Secondhand
38. Brass instruments
39. Helm direction
40. River-mouth plain
42. Poorest
44. Overly inquisitive
46. Sledder's delight
48. Leg joint
49. Gremlin's kin
50. ____ Galahad
51. Undercover man

47

ACROSS

1. Bible boat
4. Pine
8. 43,560 square feet
12. Rival
13. On vacation
14. Certain chess piece
15. Brewery beverage
16. Stargazer's aid
18. Ignited again
20. Sealed
21. Lured
25. Impresses greatly
28. Components
32. Piglet's mother
33. Whines
34. Morsel for Dobbin
35. Square dances
37. Askew
38. Alternatively
40. Play platform
43. Lounged around
47. Hive dwellers
51. December 31, e.g.
52. Carney and Linkletter
53. Said aloud
54. Canister
55. Comply with
56. Corral opening
57. Crafty

DOWN

1. Off at a distance
2. Audition goal
3. Ship's feature
4. Dull finish
5. Be obliged to pay
6. Friend
7. Needle's hole
8. Arched gallery
9. Farm structure
10. Lasso cord
11. ___ out (barely made)
17. Wineglass parts
19. "___ Impossible"
22. Cat calls
23. Seedling
24. Rigid
25. Fire remains
26. Court, as a sweetheart
27. Lamb's parent
29. At this moment
30. Pave
31. Filthy abode
33. "The Color of ___"
36. Absorb
37. Do sums
39. Passageway
40. Farce
41. Shredded
42. Starting bet
44. Rents
45. Vile
46. Declare untrue
48. Cranberry location
49. Memorable time
50. Have a snack

48

ACROSS

1. On vacation
5. Spiders' traps
9. Dry gently
12. Farm tower
13. Leave
14. Solid water
15. Catch
16. Agile
17. By means of
18. ___ milk
20. Repair
21. Moreover
23. Punching tool
24. Fidgety
25. Calculate, in a way
26. Parties
29. More profound
31. Makes into a statute
35. Most aged
37. School dance
38. Eve's home
41. Be competitive
42. "___ Which Way You Can"
43. Military land-force
44. ___ of honor
46. Shoot the breeze
47. Soft drink
48. Pesky insect
51. Be deceptive
52. Unfenced
53. Advice from a decorator
54. Aim
55. Supreme
56. If not

DOWN

1. Horse's kin
2. Come in first
3. Pie ___: 3 wds.
4. Type of exercise
5. Toward the setting sun
6. Forces out
7. Feathered friend
8. Sow's place
9. Plunged headfirst into water
10. Doing very well on
11. Small and round
19. Insignia
20. Small plateau
21. Tiny bit
22. Verse type
27. Reluctant
28. Submit a contest solution
30. "The Red ___"
32. TV station
33. Large weight unit
34. Enemy agent
36. Avoids
38. National symbol
39. Tub feature
40. Set in
44. Pout
45. Grimm villain
47. Weep
49. TV commercials
50. Foot digit

49

ACROSS

1. Baltic or Black
4. Yellow metal
8. Hawaiian gift
11. Solo of "Return of the Jedi"
12. Esteem
13. Prone
14. Notable period
15. Literary work
16. Attack!
17. Abate
19. Engrave on glass
20. The ___ and wherefores
22. Details
24. Take it easy: 2 wds.
26. Narrate
30. Vocal solos
31. Title giver
32. Bother
34. Evening meal
35. Decree
37. Eternities
38. Play sections
41. Sculptor's device
43. Is allowed to
44. Hut
45. Charged atom
48. Scribe's fluid
49. Enthusiastic
50. A pair
51. Below-average grade
52. West Pointer's force
53. To the bitter ___

DOWN

1. That girl
2. Serving of corn
3. Careful study
4. Busybody
5. Start
6. Temporary replacement
7. Like some martinis
8. Be enough
9. Heroic story
10. Seven-year ___
12. "___ So Shy"
18. Lands
19. Fugitive from prison
20. Enclose
21. Roll call response
23. List of activities
25. Like some cars
27. Rude
28. MTV watcher
29. Bungles
33. More wealthy
34. Gooey
36. Trinket
38. Within
39. Christmas candy shape
40. Toddler
42. Blue above us
44. Saratoga Springs, e.g.
46. Have
47. Beckon

50

ACROSS

1. In the know
4. Prune
8. Ski lift: hyph.
12. Lobe location
13. Ripped
14. Courageous one
15. Brief stay on a journey
17. Totter
18. Be in hock
19. Whitish gem
20. Teenager's woe
23. Andean animal
27. Travel course
29. Intensely
33. Contemptible fellow
34. Bird abodes
36. "___, though I walk . . ."
37. Shirt parts
39. Pinch playfully
41. Hosiery material
43. Betting numbers
44. Exam
47. Stir
49. Tress material
50. Modernizes
55. Unit of farmland
56. Raw minerals
57. Mouth edge
58. "How do I love ___?"
59. Slosh through water
60. Florida island

DOWN

1. Stags and bucks
2. Consume food
3. Opposite of con
4. Load cargo
5. Work of fiction
6. Deep anger
7. For every
8. Tonsils' site
9. Electronic reminder
10. Realm
11. Move on wheels
16. Emily Dickinson, e.g.
20. Crescents
21. Fossil fuel
22. Undressed
24. Rodeo rope
25. Perform onstage
26. Should
28. Jealousy
30. Spotted
31. Weighty metal
32. Chatters
35. Wiggly fish
38. Meal course
40. Lumber
42. Identified
44. "All ___ Jazz"
45. Every individual
46. Regal title
48. Medicine amount
50. Noisy dispute
51. Division of time
52. Moose's relative
53. Tell a falsehood
54. Snoop

51

ACROSS

1. Certain liquor
4. Venomous serpents
8. Plushy
12. Service point
13. "How do I love ___?"
14. Long-eared animal
15. Stitch
16. Allows
18. Kilt
20. Unexpected defeat
21. Stern
23. Shout to a matador
24. Performed a garden chore
25. Entertainer Bob ___
27. In addition
30. Chowed down
31. Woodcutter
32. Lad
33. Become firm
34. Cake layer
35. Honest
36. Neither's partner
37. Teem
39. Trickier
42. Letter's need
43. Mechanical
45. Running game
48. Small valley
49. Damp
50. Caustic stuff
51. Shade trees
52. Omelet ingredients
53. Nonetheless

DOWN

1. Step on the ___ (hurry)
2. Skater's surface
3. Old-movie feature
4. Topmost floor
5. Kind of cat
6. Animal fur
7. Look
8. Figure
9. Horse's food
10. Complimentary
11. "___ Pilot"
17. Measuring device
19. Nanny's offspring
21. Rug type
22. Lug
23. Running
26. Be in the red
27. Instantly
28. Name word
29. Changed color
31. Blizzard
35. Mr. Hanks
36. Advertising lights
38. Fronts' opposites
39. Stuffing herb
40. Pause
41. Component
42. For men only
44. Lime beverage
46. Pirate's yes
47. Comprehend

52

ACROSS

1. Cultivates
6. Horse's kin
9. Gloomy
12. Put forth
13. Block up
14. Lode's load
15. "___ My Love"
16. Hall and Oates, e.g.
17. Casino cube
18. Folk hero
20. Wanderers
22. This lady
24. Martial art
26. Obscure place
28. Emcees
32. Follow instructions
33. Pop
35. Stop!
36. Night crawlers
38. Motives
40. Aromatic spice

42. Superman's emblem
43. More taut
46. Defrost
48. Sailor's yes
49. Party mixture
51. Standards
54. Bee's follower
55. Piece of corn
56. Pay for
57. Puzzling
58. Rocker Stone
59. Poorly kept

DOWN

1. Swamp
2. Hatchet
3. Roger Ebert, e.g.
4. TV's talking horse: 2 wds.
5. Pet
6. State further
7. Steam bath
8. Not rough
9. Root beer, e.g.

10. Parched
11. Low grades
19. Cooking grease
21. Cat calls
22. Winter fall
23. Drifter
25. Provide new weapons
27. Religious songs
29. Foot-shaped device: 2 wds.
30. Cargo weights
31. Back talk
34. Think
37. Napped leathers
39. Middlemen
41. Experiment
43. Mexican snack
44. Gazed at
45. Poverty
47. Folk knowledge
50. Open with a crowbar
52. Enraged
53. Swine home

53

ACROSS

1. Hurl
5. Pond barrier
8. At any ___
12. Fix copy
13. Intense anger
14. Aware of: 2 wds.
15. Beauty spot
16. Through
17. Rectify
18. Push forward
20. Decrease
22. Hog's dinner
24. Having handles
28. Beast of burden
31. Give pleasure
33. Wall-climbing plant
34. Trouble
35. Recreation areas
36. Average grade
37. Flee the law
38. Spread
39. Be wrong
40. "Sugar and ___ . . ."
42. Hit with an open hand
44. Fruity beverage
46. Strange
50. Ewe's young
53. Sternward
55. Prom night wheels
56. Fan favorite
57. Make like a pigeon
58. European range
59. Curved roof
60. Chick's mother
61. Breather

DOWN

1. Sub, e.g.
2. Perfume
3. Fodder storage area
4. Dance movements
5. Ambassador, e.g.
6. "You ___ So Beautiful"
7. Simple
8. Latin dance
9. Mock
10. Large weight
11. "The Deep ___"
19. Slipped by
21. Honeycomb material
23. Feline sounds
25. ___ pudding
26. By any chance
27. Color changer
28. Hole punchers
29. Cleaner
30. Highway vehicle
32. Framework of bones
41. Strong wire
43. ___ bear
45. A pop
47. Mosaic need
48. Naughty kids
49. Expense
50. Topper
51. Hubbub
52. Dad's mate
54. Rival

54

ACROSS

1. Saratoga Springs et al.
5. Grass-covered ground
8. Thought
12. Attended
13. Road surfacing material
14. Close to
15. Mimicked
16. Generation
17. Student's furniture
18. Monkey's treat
20. Cutting remarks
22. Identification label: 2 wds.
24. Brittle
27. Defy orders
31. "___ Gang"
32. Slangy film
33. Beer's kin
34. Not repeated: hyph.
37. Brands
39. White edible root
41. Emcee's assistant: hyph.
44. Reveal
48. Food cooker
49. Member of the flock
51. Similar
52. Ache
53. ___ and reel
54. Fat
55. Besides
56. Heavens
57. Corrosive liquids

DOWN

1. Wound covering
2. Mama's mate
3. Blessing response
4. Family cars
5. Vapor
6. Boat paddle
7. Severe
8. Violet blue hue
9. Low in pitch
10. Life of Riley
11. Boats like Noah's
19. Doze off
21. Lived
23. Does a pressroom job
24. Bird cry
25. Flow
26. Hot temper
28. Pub counter
29. Moose's cousin
30. Affirmative answer
32. Baggage carriers
35. Sink item
36. Owns
37. Merge
38. Horrify
40. Poor
41. Struggle successfully
42. Racetrack shape
43. Barnyard females
45. Fine
46. Regal form of address
47. At loose ___
50. Chinese skillet

55

ACROSS

1. Withheld
5. Frequently, to Keats
8. Certain spice
12. Frosting user
13. Seek the affection of
14. Presidential office shape
15. Biblical pronoun
16. Foul up
17. Greases
18. Serious
20. Canoe propeller
22. Theater attendant
24. Relieved
28. Navy officer
33. "True ___"
34. Pair
35. NBC's peacock, e.g.
36. Revive
38. Jostle
39. Tailor
41. "___ Street"
45. Tangled
50. Comparable
51. Spinning toy
53. Rub clean
54. Camp abode
55. Snack
56. Eye part
57. On ___ (tense)
58. Lacking water
59. Body part

DOWN

1. Young foxes
2. Mimic
3. Skin of an orange
4. Maple or elm
5. Actor Wilson et al.
6. Dedicated to
7. Underwater weapon
8. Attitude
9. Spirited
10. Ring
11. What ___ is new?
19. Muck
21. Sleeve filler
23. Hang around
24. Fairy
25. "Love Is in the ___"
26. Date
27. Racetrack feature
29. Off one's feed
30. Actor Morrow
31. Before now
32. Deep
34. Erased
37. Glazed ___
38. Significant period
40. Unfilled
41. Quench
42. ___ out (barely made)
43. Croon
44. Poker opener
46. Exact duplicate
47. Car's "shoe"
48. Long narrative
49. Writing table
52. Rowing blade

56

ACROSS

1. To's companion
4. Majestic trees
8. System of exercise
12. Chap
13. Chablis or Chardonnay, e.g.
14. They go baa
15. Had pasta
16. "I Dream of Jeannie" actress
17. Picnic annoyances
18. Save the —— for last
20. Citrus beverages
22. Hugged
25. Map collection
29. Attracts
33. In history
34. Nonprofessional
35. Chanced
37. Glass edge
38. —— steel
40. Skiing hill
42. NBC's peacock, e.g.
43. —— tradition
45. Social grace
49. Sunbathe
52. Litter's smallest
55. Seek the affection of
56. Muscle strain
57. As the —— flies
58. Hoopla
59. —— off (started golfing)
60. Person of the hour
61. Up to this point

DOWN

1. Loose flesh
2. Fare
3. Poetic works
4. Have bills
5. Provide support to
6. Massages dough
7. Convey
8. Bread ingredient
9. To each his ——
10. Reach
11. Horse's relative
19. Not us
21. Soothing
23. Pencil top
24. Pre-Easter time
26. Michigan or Huron
27. Eons
28. Puts in grass
29. Infirmities
30. Metal fastener
31. Memo error
32. Larry, Curly, and Moe
36. Pay phone part
39. Charm
41. Jabbed
44. Overhead curve
46. Absent
47. Secret writing
48. Beep
49. Baseball item
50. High or low card
51. Female pronoun
53. Neither fish —— fowl
54. Couple

57

ACROSS

1. Landfill
5. Grabbed a chair
8. On the road
12. Spoken
13. Noteworthy period
14. Flag site
15. Gawk
16. Disturb
17. Browning or Millay
18. Describe
20. Ill temper
22. Dad's boy
23. Sailor
27. Proclaims
31. Bowling division
32. Soft drink
33. Calling device
35. Evergreen tree
36. Cancel
38. Individuals
40. Inhabit
42. Create a quilt
43. "Neither snow, ___ rain . . ."
44. Pekoe portion: 2 wds.
48. Mr. Crosby
51. Private ___
53. Manufacture
54. Mischievous
55. Wheel tooth
56. Strait-laced
57. Classify
58. Pull
59. Hankerings

DOWN

1. Portal
2. Force along
3. Shopping place
4. Gratify
5. In ___ heaven
6. "Chances ___"
7. Cabs
8. Seem
9. Seek the love of
10. Beer's kin
11. However
19. Sub's missile
21. Umpire's cousin
24. BLT spread
25. Grace ending
26. Facts
27. Impersonator
28. Irritated
29. Vacation hot spots
30. Soak up
34. Emergency funds: 2 wds.
37. Not married
39. Boggy
41. Assemble
45. Uncovered
46. Like
47. Valuable stones
48. Play the ponies
49. ___ League school
50. Small bite
52. "It Had to Be ___"

58

ACROSS

1. Headed
4. Hit
8. Blizzard stuff
12. Zoo attraction
13. Nocturnal insect
14. Control
15. Attack!
16. Tad
17. Superior to
18. Grimace
20. Slope
22. Named in a will
24. Not a ___ to stand on
25. President's no
28. Floor model
30. Deadly snake
33. Make
35. Magazine bigwig
37. Sprinted
38. Thread for knitting
40. Depend
41. Peak
43. Mobile starter
45. Shrimp, e.g.
48. Emcee's speech, shortly
52. Deal
53. Meaning
55. Emulate Coolio
56. Land amid water
57. Chair ___
58. Bitter resentment
59. Bubblegummer
60. Choice word
61. Guys

DOWN

1. Lad's girl
2. Long heroic poem
3. Art ___
4. Grin
5. Pursue
6. Outfit
7. "Younger ___ Springtime"
8. Woman's wrap
9. Plot a course for
10. Harbinger
11. Existed
19. Stop, to Dobbin
21. Insensitive person
23. Concept
25. Certain tape player: abbr.
26. Period of time
27. Octopus's arm
29. Entree listing
31. "Do, re, mi, fa, ___ . . ."
32. Use a crowbar
34. Spelling error
36. Press
39. Certain tire
42. Again and again
44. Type of match
45. Rotisserie part
46. Relax
47. Folklore giant
49. Cut to size
50. Uncommon
51. Honest
54. Female sib

59

ACROSS

1. Wilted
5. Short reminder
9. Fitness center
12. Egg-shaped
13. Absent
14. In what manner?
15. No longer are
16. Florida islands
17. Jungle animal
18. Flower jar
20. Calmed
22. Keats poem
24. Push forward
27. Decaying
29. Moralistic story
33. Brainchild
34. Hair spray alternative
35. "Thunder ___"
36. Tyke
38. Surrounded by
39. Minute point
41. Stinging insect

42. Change color, again
45. Nomad's abode
47. Night before Christmas
48. Signal hello
51. Ins and ___
54. Needle's kin
55. Source of energy
56. Woodwind instrument
57. Sneaky
58. Evergreen plants
59. Preserved

DOWN

1. Close to the bottom
2. "___ Got Sixpence"
3. Aroused astonishment
4. Not guilty, e.g.
5. Manufacturer
6. Lamb's mama
7. Merry month
8. Pearl's place
9. Fraud

10. Vatican official
11. Deeply impressed
19. Have a look-see
21. Warning
22. Eliminate
23. Flightless bird
25. Met musical
26. Chum
28. Papa
30. TV, slangily: 2 wds.
31. Bowling alley
32. On ___ (tense)
34. Come and ___ it!
37. Margin
38. Tavern order
40. Individual things
42. Agts.
43. Something wicked
44. Refuse
46. Recess
49. Finished a meal
50. Promise solemnly
52. On ___ of the world
53. Film location

60

ACROSS

1. Gamblers' numbers
5. Deuces
9. Fitness club
12. Blubber
13. Beg
14. Religious woman
15. Like some lingerie
16. Powerful wind
17. Sculpture, e.g.
18. Prove human
19. Public
20. Bind
21. Start golfing: 2 wds.
24. Play chapters
25. Restoration
28. Wary
29. Harbor town
31. Average mark
33. Fixes
36. Parka
37. Small waterway
39. Road depression
40. Teamster's rig
43. By means of
44. 21, e.g.
45. Felled
46. Sandwich shop
47. Scratch
48. Chablis or sake
49. Press
50. Meddle
51. Seven-card ——
52. Nothing but

DOWN

1. Small hooter
2. More precious
3. Edict
4. Secret watcher
5. Rope-pulling contest: 3 wds.
6. Enfold
7. Stare
8. Discovered
9. Grab
10. Innocence
11. Poker bets
22. Start
23. Admission price
24. Out of bed
26. Tarzan's chum
27. Uneven
30. Informant
31. Mountain lion
32. Restaurant
34. Worship
35. Ship worker
36. Muscle spasm
38. Augusta's locale
40. Woodworkers' tools
41. Departure
42. List of restaurant dishes
46. Not well lit

61

ACROSS

1. Nevertheless
4. Fountain drink
8. Take out, as text
12. ___ of a kind (unique)
13. Couples
14. Balanced
15. TV announcements
16. Foot unit
17. Forward
18. Entire
20. Sleeveless garments
21. Seal's limb
25. Weight
28. Rattles
32. Rower's need
33. Liberace's instrument
34. Knock
35. Nova Scotia, e.g.
37. Military
38. Saintly
40. Sufficient
43. Pile
47. Bargain
48. Lyric poems
51. Delivery truck
52. Dunce
53. Humdinger
54. Bitter resentment
55. Swing
56. Capitol roof
57. Mountain moisture

DOWN

1. Vessel
2. Remove fasteners
3. Trial
4. Silent
5. Hold title to
6. Snow White's pal
7. Smoker's evidence
8. Dry wilderness
9. Nights before celebrations
10. Fasting season
11. Concludes
19. Fore's partner
20. Reject, as a bill
22. Cake topper
23. Position
24. Committee
25. Leap
26. Sound organ
27. To's associate
29. Drop the ball
30. Flock father
31. Catch a glimpse of
33. Evergreen
36. Hollow between hills
37. Play a role
39. Edition
40. Remarks further
41. Cat's cry
42. Mama's fellow
44. Eager
45. Attention
46. Recognized
48. Stale
49. Sonny and Cher, once
50. Large tree

62

ACROSS

1. Hand covering
6. Wooden box
11. Ages
13. Wipes off
14. Regard favorably
15. Camera attachments
16. Existed
17. Soldier's weapon
19. Gawk at
20. Stick with this
25. Overdue
28. Cure
29. Beams of light
30. Society miss
32. Snaky swimmers
33. Land parcel
34. Love affair
36. The things here
38. Inspired
39. Country estate
41. James Bond, e.g.
44. Make less hard
48. Undivided
50. Pungent bulbs
51. Become darker
52. Sired
53. Grates

DOWN

1. Enlarged
2. Ms. Bonet
3. Selects
4. Sign of triumph
5. Vigor
6. Inch along
7. Hightailed it
8. Wild donkey
9. Informal shirt
10. Superman's initial
12. Grinned
13. Building addition
18. Part of FBI
19. Desert stops
21. In advance
22. Beheld
23. Bath powder
24. When all —— fails . . .
25. Phooey's kin
26. Every individual
27. Old stringed instrument
31. Played ninepins
35. More unkind
37. Noteworthy happening
40. Outs' opposites
41. Uses a straw
42. Get ready
43. Strong desires
44. Cry
45. "—— Life to Live"
46. Often-dried fruit
47. Furthermore
49. Herbal beverage

63

ACROSS

1. Track circuit
4. Amounts
8. Snooty person
12. Tanker cargo
13. Group of three
14. Small skin hole
15. "— to the West Wind"
16. Pointed out
18. Rockers — Jam
20. Sick
21. Building extension
23. Map collection
28. Paddles
31. Headset part
34. Heroic
35. Common ailment
36. Pace
37. Subtracted
39. Bucks
40. Scornful smile
41. Lessen

43. Wise bird
46. College paper
50. Comfortable seat: 2 wds.
55. Put to good —
56. Sprain result
57. Perfume
58. Wiggly sea creature
59. 11th grader
60. Mimicking bird
61. Faucet

DOWN

1. Part of a bow
2. Official assistant
3. Reason
4. Silent
5. Coffeepot
6. Skirt type
7. Ground
8. Mountain resort
9. "— Without My Daughter"
10. Gold source
11. Sleeping spot
17. Thunderous sound

19. Save
22. Exited
24. Beats strongly
25. Bank deal
26. Poker word
27. Catches sight of
28. Cincinnati's nine
29. Ready for business
30. Expansive
32. Bitter brew
33. Uncivil
38. Gator's cousin
42. Yogi — of baseball
44. Which person?
45. "— Sings the Blues"
47. Fat
48. Cruising
49. High-pitched cry
50. Have breakfast
51. Serve for a point
52. This woman
53. Longing
54. Charged atom

64

ACROSS

1. Evils
5. Spring bloom
9. Baby's dinner wear
12. Kitten sound
13. Sand hill
14. Master
15. Plumbing part
16. Preoccupied
18. Friendly nation
20. Not as much
21. Picture
24. Dove's call
26. Fishing pole
27. Later
33. Up in years
34. Monster
35. Pool stick
36. Frantic
38. Curved bone
39. Equip with weapons
40. Broker
42. Day's beginning
45. Out of action
47. Mimic
50. On the summit
54. Chip enhancer
55. Facts
56. Took the ferry
57. The "I" in TGIF
58. Obstacle
59. Ladder rung

DOWN

1. Mischievous tyke
2. Hawaiian gift
3. Trim
4. Perspire
5. Religious figurine
6. Red stone
7. Stand-___
8. Get it?
9. Diamond feature
10. Frosts
11. Flower plots
17. Slacken
19. Lazy person
21. Spur
22. Opening
23. Bettor's numbers
24. Lincoln coin
25. Trying experience
28. Solid
29. Chinese beverage
30. Estate unit
31. Destruction
32. Something owed
37. Huff and puff
41. Mechanical parts
42. Type of skirt
43. Fail to include
44. Slits
45. Small bit
46. Pull
48. Promos
49. Sun-bronzed
51. Toddler
52. Keats poem
53. Vitality

65

ACROSS

1. "___ Old Man"
5. Specks
9. ___ and gown
12. "Roxie ___"
13. Fixed quantity
14. Be in the red
15. Healing plant
16. Scorch
17. Adult males
18. Resident
20. Wander
22. Broom's wet kin
23. Heavenly visitors
26. Fine glassware
30. Aladdin's friend
31. Shade of color
32. Yuletide drink
34. Crow call
35. Adjust
38. Rags
41. Interval
43. Deface
44. Approach
45. Beermaker
49. "___ Belongs to Me"
51. Earth
53. Change address
54. Average
55. Raced
56. Baker's need
57. Some are personal
58. Went in haste
59. Remainder

DOWN

1. "___ Girl"
2. Golfer Irwin
3. Household appliance
4. Cooks with vapor
5. Cleaning crew's utensil
6. Washington bill
7. Elegant headgear
8. Mighty
9. Begin
10. Fearful wonder
11. Farm enclosure
19. "Ask ___ what your country . . ."
21. Generation
24. Fibber
25. Hems a skirt
26. Gent
27. Boorish
28. Longing people
29. Fortune
33. Took a risk
36. Crusted dessert
37. Browns bread
39. Pave
40. Quake
42. Sag
46. Knitted
47. Nights preceding
48. Landlord's concern
49. Resort for dieters
50. "Mary ___ a little lamb . . ."
52. Great wrath

66

ACROSS

1. Bowling target
4. Empty of water
8. Lug
12. Great anger
13. Burn reliever
14. Knitting material
15. Skier's line
16. Granted the use of
17. Encourage
18. Nonsupporters
20. Fogs
21. Mexican menu items
25. Keats poems
28. Flexible materials
32. Negative connector
33. Stow away
34. Dove's call
35. Paint-removing tools
37. Guard
38. Confused state
40. Knight's protection
43. Powdery
47. Intend
48. Written comment
51. Compensated player
52. Better half
53. Opera highlight
54. "___ House"
55. Chooses
56. Fruit cover
57. Ess follower

DOWN

1. Pocket bread
2. Potential steel
3. Small salamander
4. Light wood
5. Pub brew
6. Charged atom
7. Said yes to
8. Office employee
9. Rowing items
10. Harness-racing gait
11. Make ___ meet (get by)
19. Possessive pronoun
20. Interlock
22. Parking lot device
23. Alert
24. Rope
25. Offs' opposites
26. Physician, briefly
27. Make a misstep
29. Rink surface
30. Debate side
31. Grass section
33. San Antonio player
36. Makes up (for)
37. Common ailment
39. Model
40. Bullets, for short
41. You ___ what you sow
42. Actor Damon
44. Dot
45. ___ or false
46. Olden days
48. Sack out
49. Valuable rock
50. Neckwear

67

ACROSS

1. Group
5. In fashion
8. Narrow cut
12. Mocker
13. Have creditors
14. Commotion: hyph.
15. Mother
16. Feeling rotten
17. Competently
18. Chooses
20. Wigwams' cousins
22. Spaghetti topping
24. Apron part
26. Hive-dwelling insect
27. Picket ___
31. Future sign
33. Young bug
35. Totter
36. Rainy month
38. Sticky substance
40. Emerald, e.g.
41. Nurturing
44. Grouchy
47. Average
50. Lounge
51. Freezer cube
53. Fairy-tale beast
54. A woodwind
55. Convent resident
56. Cribbage needs
57. Gaze
58. Capture
59. Pullover shirts

DOWN

1. All the ___ (nevertheless)
2. October's stone
3. Recall
4. Track
5. Dampen
6. Hooter
7. "___ Dawn" (Reddy song)
8. Swingline product
9. Earring's location
10. Not busy
11. Dolls and blocks, e.g.
19. Check
21. Mischievous sprite
23. Ecru
24. ___ constrictor (snake)
25. Naughty child
28. Dressing gown
29. Letter before dee
30. Nightmare street of film
32. More agile
34. Plague
37. Chemist's room
39. Single
42. Fastening with rope
43. Care for an orphan
44. Hoofbeat sound
45. Royal garment
46. Soothing plant
48. Advise
49. Chaos
52. Guiding suggestion

68

ACROSS

1. Pull heavily
5. Fuss
8. Large mop
12. Particle
13. Cow chow
14. Cover up
15. Lemon skin
16. Unequal: hyph.
18. Ancient instrument
20. Lock of hair
21. Lustrous fabric
24. Middle Eastern bread
25. Archer's weapon
26. Ventilate
27. Sopping
30. Broadway sign
31. Spanish hooray
32. Tar
33. River obstruction
34. Ailing
35. Backpacks
36. Tie
38. Most pleasant
39. Timepiece
41. Reserved
42. Melon variety
44. Large vases
48. Computer operator
49. Not offs
50. Chess piece
51. Disorderly state
52. Timid
53. Fidgety

DOWN

1. Immerse briefly
2. Fish eggs
3. Had pasta
4. Spanish treasure ship
5. Oak's nut
6. Desert hill
7. Lyric poem
8. Polo ___
9. Alert: 2 wds.
10. Sweet drinks
11. Cots
17. Move
19. Evergreen shrub
21. Desert covering
22. District
23. Brass instruments
24. Filled dessert
26. "___ I Need"
28. Nights before
29. Sample
31. Archaic
32. Mental image
34. Like writing fluid
35. Body joint
37. Bakery workers
38. Gossipy
39. Pal
40. Be an also-ran
41. Gambling game
43. Medic
45. Baton
46. Eggy drink
47. Star's locale

69

ACROSS

1. Not at home
5. Health centers
9. '50s dance party
12. Building's location
13. Radial, e.g.
14. Anger
15. Beef dish
16. Quick look: hyph.
18. March proudly
20. Harmful insect
21. Hill builder
24. Baseball official
26. Verdict renderers
28. Movie house
32. Pass into law
33. Demon
34. Say again
36. Enlarges
37. Good sense
39. "Blame It on ___"
40. Zone
43. Drab
45. Crooked
47. "Jagged ___"
51. Pasture female
52. Reside
53. Soap-making substances
54. Compass point: abbr.
55. Suggestive glance
56. Allows

DOWN

1. Pack animal
2. Clever humor
3. Had supper
4. Coniferous shrubs
5. Tempests
6. GI's poster
7. North Pole region
8. "___ How She Runs"
9. Center of activity
10. Valuable lodes
11. Sassy
17. Unwrapped
19. Pond resident
21. Not quite closed
22. In the buff
23. Jog
25. Going by bus
27. Met offerings
29. By any chance
30. Kind of skirt
31. To boot
35. Scottish boy
36. Amazement
38. Strainer
40. Pub orders
41. Moves a skiff
42. Fencing tool
44. Cry out
46. ___ at ease
48. Artificial color
49. Earn
50. Road bend

70

ACROSS

1. High cards
5. Card-game cry
8. Picks
12. Long skirt
13. Stir
14. Hockey score
15. Small devils
16. Floral garland
17. Walk-on
18. Letter after cee
19. Fixed a ceiling
21. Christmas singer
23. Moisturizers
25. America's Cup competitor
30. Felt obligated
31. Halt!
32. Below
34. Answered
37. Cold manner
39. Cargo ship
43. Ease off
46. Enjoy a book
47. "___ Day Will Come"
48. Run away
49. "Duke of ___"
50. Periodical, for short
51. Let
52. Or ___ (threat)
53. Fabric layer
54. Evens' opposites

DOWN

1. At the center of
2. Arrived
3. Anticipated
4. Female sib
5. Ten-___ hat
6. Dreams
7. Unpleasant sound
8. Grimm heavy
9. Moneyless
10. Fictitious story
11. Toboggan
19. In support of
20. Attempt
22. General's helper
23. Baseballer Gehrig
24. "My ___ Private Idaho"
26. Piercing tools
27. Clearly shaped
28. Gardener's tool
29. Tiny bit
33. Big truck
34. Ceremony
35. Vitality
36. Apiece
38. Bite down
39. At no charge
40. Sincere
41. Hearing organs
42. At a standstill
44. River curve
45. Antes
48. To's opposite

71

ACROSS

1. Potato snack
5. Parsley, sage, or thyme
9. Use a chair
12. Went by train
13. Verbal
14. Sock front
15. Evils
16. "I Remember ___"
17. "___ Not Unusual"
18. Ladybug, e.g.
20. Unit of gold content
22. Bottle-cap remover
25. Blond shade
28. Delight
29. Young woman
33. Goad
35. Curved line
36. Beast's neck gear
37. Heroic narrative
38. Finished together
40. Veto
41. Fondue essential
43. Male duck
46. Deceitful
51. Scurried
52. Totally confused
55. Teen affliction
56. Gallery exhibit
57. Kitty sigh
58. Lean
59. Informal shirt
60. Active
61. Matched pairs

DOWN

1. Baby's furniture
2. Doughnut center
3. Loiter
4. Bother
5. Batter's location: 2 wds.
6. Historical period
7. Butt into
8. Actress Amanda ___
9. Rustle
10. Pinch
11. Quiz
19. Flight record
21. Land force
23. Strange
24. Required
25. Wild donkey
26. Place for a workout
27. Embrace
30. Charged atom
31. Descend Mt. Snow
32. Gender
34. Hat stand
39. Hideout
42. Loads
43. Darn!
44. Seldom seen
45. Contribute a share
47. Erodes
48. Hurt
49. Purl's counterpart
50. Desires
53. Dine in the evening
54. Misstate

72

ACROSS

1. Cultivate
5. Year portions
9. Bar drink
12. Went by auto
13. Burn soother
14. Vast timespan
15. Says further
16. Sleuth Hammer
17. Cow's chew
18. River-mouth plain
20. Lamp spirit
22. Nutritious bean
23. Container
25. Spat
28. Besides
30. At all
31. "___ Edition"
35. Cure
37. Carry on
38. Peppy
40. Hero's tale
41. Put to good ___
42. Weaken
45. Diagram
48. Tango or waltz
50. Majestic tree
52. So long, in Soho: 2 wds.
54. Evaluate
55. Grape or orange drink
56. Metallic deposits
57. Riding whip
58. Not against
59. Bonus
60. Not his

DOWN

1. Diploma recipients
2. Cattle-roping show
3. Peculiarly
4. East's opposite
5. Block up
6. Straightens
7. Oxen harness
8. Looked at
9. Get
10. Second person
11. ___ of the line
19. Mastered
21. Bit of info
24. Beerlike brews
26. Fueled
27. Cook in fat
29. Goofs up
31. Rage
32. Brief doze
33. Slight giggle
34. Hunger
36. Gazed upon
39. Green club
42. Pitfall
43. Stage performer
44. Looks at
46. At the summit
47. Exceptional
49. Overhead curve
50. Blockhead
51. Commotion
53. Solicit

73

ACROSS

1. Colt's mom
5. Throb painfully
9. Food for dipping
12. Steel source
13. Large diving bird
14. Shade of color
15. Give temporarily
16. Australian birds
17. Be mistaken
18. Cowboy's need
20. Dried plum
22. Swimsuit component
24. Some noblemen
27. Public notices
30. Banish
32. Borscht vegetable
33. Use a straw
34. Winding curves
36. Bering, e.g.
37. ___ the peace
39. Glimmer
40. Attempt
41. Snatch
43. Solemn lyric poem
44. Attracted
46. Snapshot
51. Summer quencher
53. You ___ what you sow
55. Similar
56. Masculine title
57. Kill a bill
58. Gold fabric
59. "___ So Shy"
60. Parodied
61. Corrosive liquids

DOWN

1. Grain grinder
2. Sector
3. Glass and Moody
4. Wraps up
5. Hops beverage
6. Sympathetic
7. 60 minutes
8. Develop
9. Most transparent
10. Possessive pronoun
11. For every
19. Wind instrument
21. Snatch
23. Hustle
25. Malicious look
26. Command to Fido
27. Probes
28. Food plan
29. Lawbreaking drivers
31. Look after
35. Pace
38. Golfer's goal
42. Immature insect stage
45. Sob
47. TV's Monty ___
48. Give approval to
49. Clock
50. "The Defiant ___"
51. Smoker's evidence
52. Game cube
54. Bean shell

74

ACROSS

1. Chop
4. Flutter
8. Spinning toys
12. Natural resource
13. Guitarlike instrument
14. Egg-shaped
15. Attendance
17. Hereditary unit
18. Per
19. Rowed
20. Fashionable
23. Religious song
25. Roster
26. Excuses
31. At sea
34. Powerhouse
35. Stab
36. Place for a kiss
37. Chalet feature
40. To boot
41. Mild oaths
45. Church response
47. Vogue
48. Kitchen appliances
52. Flat
53. Husk
54. Scoundrel
55. Joins
56. Does arithmetic
57. At least one

DOWN

1. Dance
2. Blunder
3. Petite
4. Market or circus
5. Midday meal
6. Scratchy
7. Kicking gadget
8. Nero's attire
9. Completed
10. Window unit
11. Arctic transport
16. Zone
19. Just
20. Thunderous sound
21. Stereo: hyph.
22. Florida Key, e.g.
24. Irate
27. Away from the shore
28. Ladle
29. Mischievous kids
30. Not bad: hyph.
32. Expert pilots
33. Iced brew
38. Legitimate
39. Make right
41. Sketched
42. Carry on
43. Like some wine
44. Hamilton bills
46. At loose ___
48. Halter
49. Division of history
50. Bolted
51. Hog's place

75

ACROSS

1. Woman's shoe
5. Leaders
8. Resounded
12. Confused
13. —— the mark
14. Clarinet's kin
15. Take five
16. Kindest
18. —— and field
20. Walks through water
21. Earphones
25. Free (of)
28. Make ready
29. Imprint with acid
33. Point-scoring serve
34. November's gem
36. Shade
37. Evergreen plants
39. Fountain treat
40. Definitely!
41. Fake
44. Snow building
47. Chowed down
51. Chime to announce visitors
55. Plunged
56. Oaf
57. Hive-building insect
58. TV's Carey
59. Concludes
60. "The —— Chill"
61. Wishes

DOWN

1. Actor's role
2. Operator
3. Flat-topped formation
4. Mend
5. "—— Impossible"
6. This instant
7. Glimpse
8. Revolve
9. Still asleep
10. Smeller
11. Understands
17. Member of the flock
19. Retained
22. Came up
23. Terminal
24. Shovel's cousin
25. Beam of light
26. Glacier material
27. Morning wetness
30. Old pronoun
31. Stage reminder
32. "For —— a jolly . . ."
35. Author Grey
38. Hockey and baseball
42. Filch
43. Mommy's mate
44. At leisure
45. Mobster's man
46. Earsplitting
48. Ripped
49. Divisible by two
50. Latest word
52. —— tide
53. Orchid necklace
54. Shake a —— (hurry)

76

ACROSS

1. Stop, to Dobbin
5. Workout site
8. Coral structure
12. Alters in length
13. Circle section
14. Roof part
15. Unrefined minerals
16. Foot digit
17. Attracted
18. List of restaurant dishes
19. Observe secretly
21. Jam
25. Witness again
29. Heedful
33. ___ through the nose
34. Place
35. Military helpers
36. Apply
37. European mountain
38. Beasts
40. Film star George C. ___
42. Swine food
43. Deadly reptile
45. Massages
49. Has a mortgage
52. Noteworthy time
55. Said aloud
56. "I ___ Forget You"
57. Sink down
58. Gawk at
59. Rich deposit
60. Couple
61. Mounted on a peg

DOWN

1. "For ___ the Bell Tolls"
2. Classroom response
3. Bird of ill ___
4. Guess
5. Made a lap
6. In favor of
7. Masters
8. Tint again
9. Lobe's place
10. Night before a holiday
11. Not many
20. Immediately
22. Passes into law
23. Move
24. A triangle has three
26. Goad
27. Rest
28. "Lyin' ___"
29. Cry of dismay
30. Fine powder
31. Memo error
32. Schnitzel meat
39. Pull weeds
41. Sample
44. Gnat, for one
46. Suggest strongly
47. Bundle
48. Husky's load
49. Bird of prey
50. Flirt with
51. Rearmost part
53. Green
54. In the past

77

ACROSS

1. Adult boy
4. Ship's pronoun
7. Coffee variety
12. Become mature
13. Female bird
14. Moral
15. Small watercraft
17. "___ Goes Another Love Song"
18. Up to the time that
20. Meadow mowers
21. Type of tea
24. Back part
26. "___ Breaky Heart"
27. Panic
28. Astonishment
31. Follower
33. Bug
35. Timespan
36. Meaning
38. Weeder
39. Gawk at
40. Inclined planes
41. Greatest amount
44. Metric quart
46. Leaves out
48. Fasteners
52. Brawl
53. Snakelike swimmer
54. Not me
55. Grunt
56. Evaporate
57. Ease off

DOWN

1. Ruin
2. Before now
3. ___ York
4. Shed light
5. "Body ___"
6. Whole
7. Faced
8. Additional
9. Grind with the teeth
10. Employ
11. High cards
16. Floating markers
19. Vaulted
21. Measured tread
22. Sound reverberation
23. Genghis ___
25. Common verb
27. Luxury
28. Small particle
29. Shed tears
30. Gets it wrong
32. Breakfast item
34. Clever
37. Grasped
39. River creature
40. Respond
41. Dads' wives
42. Indication of future events
43. Farm structure
45. Cake layer
47. Ready, ___, go
49. Look over
50. Actor Lowe
51. Hoagy

78

ACROSS

1. Rearward, nautically
4. Dotty
8. Boring tool
11. Snivel
12. Colder
14. Anti's opposite
15. Do better than
16. Gladiator's spot
17. Expel
18. Lazy person
20. Narrative writing
22. Art ___
24. Patients
26. Spoken
27. Obeys
28. Skipper's kitchen
30. Stage lines
34. Madison Avenue employee
36. "The Farmer in the ___"
37. Making a touchdown
40. Homely
41. Depend
42. Church leader
45. Rodent pest
46. Possessor
48. Flock member
51. Breakfasted
52. Cowboy show
53. Eternity
54. For each
55. O.K. Corral gunfighter
56. Turf

DOWN

1. Portray
2. "To and ___"
3. Ordinary
4. Channel changer
5. Land division
6. Savage
7. Finger count
8. Chef's garment
9. Bracelet's site
10. Mineral deposits
13. Rafter's thrill
19. Bills
21. Remains
22. Hound
23. Distinctive period
25. Sparse
27. Anthem
29. Newspaper chief
31. Units of heat
32. House annex
33. Rocker Stone
35. Meeting schedule
37. Leather thong
38. Packing box
39. Exterior
43. Impolite look
44. Small quantity
47. Unhappiness
49. Flirt with
50. Objective

79

ACROSS

1. Switch
5. Diamond or pearl
8. Blacken with flame
12. Small amount
13. Actress Gabor
14. Opening
15. Adolescent
16. Young bug
17. Atop
18. Lived
20. Root vegetable
21. Carnival
24. Ease off
26. Bar beverage
27. Few and ___ between
29. Fibbing
33. "___ Impossible"
34. Blaze
36. Buck's companion
37. Demolish
39. Afternoon meal
40. Give permission
41. ___ your request
43. Entry
45. Bargain-hunt
48. Scratchy
50. Mama's man
51. Barrel
52. Grouchy person
56. White House office shape
57. "The Hairy ___"
58. Doily
59. Snitch
60. Preceded
61. Stared at

DOWN

1. Take a load off
2. Heartache
3. Gobbled
4. Bamboo-eating mammal
5. Patton's rank
6. Cruel
7. Not glossy
8. Plump
9. Keep expectations
10. Sunburn soother
11. Apartment expense
19. Equivocate
21. Fishing lure
22. ___ saxophone
23. Relish
25. Whitener
28. Scoundrel
30. Jobless
31. Negative responses
32. Attains
35. Responded
38. Horrify
42. Challenger
44. Two-wheeled vehicle
45. X marks it
46. Own
47. Milky jewel
49. Cassette, e.g.
53. Beam
54. Perfect serve
55. Place for flowers

80

ACROSS

1. Ballet costume
5. Shorten
8. Choir member
12. Ready for business
13. Clinging vine
14. Close tightly
15. Heavy weight units
16. Grown boys
17. Ilk
18. Result
20. Tavern order
22. Dock dwellers
25. Standing
29. Supplies
33. Icky stuff
34. Intense anger
35. Bills of fare
36. Mine's output
37. Afternoon party
38. Locations
40. More domesticated
42. Mailed
43. Cloud's locale
45. Gown fabric
49. Unreturnable tennis serves
52. Fore's counterpart
55. Revere's midnight journey
56. Nero's garment
57. Seek the love of
58. Personnel
59. Irritable
60. Butterfly trap
61. Warmth

DOWN

1. Carry
2. Versed in
3. Wallet bills
4. Hesitant
5. That guy
6. Christmas ___
7. Mimicking bird
8. Inquisitive one
9. Waikiki wreath
10. Handbag hue
11. Opposite of young
19. Set aside
21. Decreases
23. Came out even
24. Smooths
26. Personality parts
27. Nucleus
28. Foot appendages
29. Catcher's glove
30. Location
31. Mets, e.g.
32. Attract
39. Collar stiffener
41. Short paper
44. Exhibit boredom
46. Lose interest
47. Notion
48. Small salamander
49. Gulped down
50. Cape ___
51. Omelet necessity
53. Rival
54. Youngster

81

ACROSS

1. Iranian ruler, once
5. Covered
9. Restaurant bill
12. Maui dance
13. Drifter
14. Chopper
15. Cry out
16. Potent particle
17. Sick
18. On behalf of
20. Purple
22. Commuter's vehicle
25. Important
27. Garb
29. Scarlett ___
33. ___ over (erupt)
34. Particle
36. Legendary
37. Log
39. Revitalize
41. Revoke officially
43. Blue yonder
44. Minister
47. Seedy bread
49. Frozen water
50. John XXIII, e.g.
52. Having talent
56. Historic period
57. Always
58. In ___ (futilely)
59. Place
60. Current events
61. Watched

DOWN

1. Timid
2. Tint
3. Every bit
4. 50%
5. Scorched
6. Building parcel
7. Superior
8. Game tile with dots
9. Pursue
10. Automobile part
11. Conveyor ___
19. "___ Town" (Wilder play)
21. Different
22. Slugger Ruth
23. "___ the Roof": 2 wds.
24. Turning barbecue skewer
26. Shine
28. Careful
30. Tarzan's pals
31. Hazard
32. Sore
35. Carriers
38. Unlock again
40. Travel by plane
42. Show to be true
44. Filled pastries
45. Measure of farmland
46. Pants part
48. Chalet feature
51. Cathedral sight
53. Inlet
54. Tell a falsehood
55. Conclude

82

ACROSS

1. Tiny green plants
5. Skiing surface
9. Break in a barrier
12. Initial stake
13. Ebb ___
14. Excitement
15. Look at quickly
16. Veteran: hyph.
18. Pants' parts
19. Spider's spinning
20. Eagle's dwelling
21. Enthusiasm
23. Rearward, nautically
25. Master
27. Trains' pathways
33. Loser
34. Dad's brother
35. Filled pastry crust
36. Most rapid
38. Chapel bench
39. Diamond, e.g.
40. Lancelot or Galahad
42. Kind of rug
45. Bonfire residue
48. Hurl
51. Tape holder
53. Level
54. Pub specialty
55. Have on, as clothing
56. Mother, informally
57. Feathered stole
58. "The ___ of Night"
59. Mistake

DOWN

1. Alda's series
2. Fairy-tale beginning
3. Onrush of cattle
4. Touch, e.g.
5. Put on cargo
6. Cleo's river
7. Eccentric people
8. Soggy
9. "The Crying ___"
10. Grape and lime drinks
11. Harbor town
17. "___ each life . . ."
22. Overly modest one
24. Worries
25. Magazine fillers
26. Cooking measure
28. Like cartoons
29. Decorate a cake
30. Permission
31. "___ Hard" (Willis film)
32. Perform needlework
37. Hens' outlay
41. List entries
42. Wound cover
43. Angelic headlight
44. Cruising
46. Doe's mate
47. "___ Comes the Sun"
49. 18-wheeler
50. Click
52. Ram's counterpart

83

ACROSS

1. Dogs' feet
5. Throb painfully
9. Passing fashion
12. Civil disorder
13. Conflict for two
14. Be deceptive
15. Scent
16. Wild attempt
17. Bitter brew
18. Unger of "The Odd Couple"
20. Condemn
22. Compress
25. Lingers
28. Mimicked
32. Lower joint
33. Ruby-colored
34. Swiss song
36. Topaz, e.g.
37. Forewarning
39. Pasta tubes
41. Forbidden items: hyph.
43. ___ conquers all
44. Small branch
46. Caper
50. Hawaiian gift
52. Sand
55. Mexican meal
56. Morsel for Dobbin
57. Rabbitlike animal
58. Hymn ender
59. Make an effort
60. Toddler
61. Not as much

DOWN

1. College teacher, shortly
2. ___-de-camp
3. Cashmere, e.g.
4. Tough
5. Sales pitches
6. Slit
7. River source
8. Nudge
9. Wading bird
10. Be unwell
11. Below-average grade
19. Medical photo: hyph.
21. Large tree
23. Source of energy
24. Bravery award
26. Youth
27. Trucker's vehicle
28. Press clothes
29. Note
30. Self
31. Art ___
35. Volcano output
38. Immediately
40. Apartment, e.g.
42. Power of seeing
45. Confederate color
47. Domesticate
48. Frozen desserts
49. Swindles
50. Parcel
51. Corn piece
53. Irritate
54. Comfy shirt

84

ACROSS

1. Kind of poker
5. Decorate a tree
9. Milk source
12. Askew
13. Disrespectful
14. Fruity refresher
15. Placard
16. Not deserved
18. Swipes
20. Feasted
21. Silver, e.g.
23. Surrounded by
27. Cherished
30. Hopeful
31. Maven
32. Bread ingredient
35. Pub brew
36. Rug type
38. Serving tray
40. Divan, e.g.
41. Distinctive manner
42. Wharf rodent
44. Close
48. Refined
52. Apple part
53. Natural mineral
54. Till bills
55. At the top
56. Network
57. "Green —— and Ham"
58. Church furniture

DOWN

1. Lip
2. Taunt
3. Motivate
4. Powerhouse
5. Board member
6. Flee
7. Flawless
8. Beef or pork
9. Container
10. Shelley offering
11. Join in marriage
17. Bring up
19. Tariff
22. Adjust
24. Castle ditch
25. Bit of land
26. Hair colorist
27. Freshwater game fish
28. Canyon's answer
29. Fall faller
33. Cunning
34. Fable
37. Actor Cooper
39. Tempest in a ——
41. Hornet's revenge
43. Soothing plant
45. Lasso cord
46. Ridge over the eye
47. Yearnings
48. Deep in pitch
49. Have being
50. Young society woman
51. Nail holder

85

ACROSS

1. Scram
5. Powerful particle
9. Bread for pastrami
12. Bend
13. Not quite ten
14. Paddle's kin
15. Used up
16. MTV viewer
17. Health center
18. Address
20. Certainly!
22. ___-and-hers
24. Recedes
27. Morsel
30. Bedridden
31. Mature
32. Freezer abundance
33. Wash
35. "Peggy ___ Got Married"
36. Hammerhead, e.g.
38. Deer's kin
39. Skirt border
40. Savior
41. Friend
42. Stirs
45. Took it easy
50. Hired vehicle
52. "For ___ the Bell Tolls"
54. Volcano flow
55. Fuel
56. Folk legends
57. Public
58. Keats work
59. Garden starter
60. Foe of the "Titanic"

DOWN

1. Hangs low
2. Farm harvest
3. Complexion woe
4. "Of ___ I Sing"
5. Insect home
6. Gift for Dad
7. Wallet stuffers
8. List of options
9. Flowering shrub
10. Talk noisily
11. Significant period
19. Baby bird
21. In the ___ (losing money)
23. Snooze
25. Out of the ___
26. Derive
27. Entree
28. Dull pain
29. Endurable
31. Foot-to-leg joint
34. Terrified
37. Slender pole
43. Wise old birds
44. Brake part
46. Untidy person
47. Measuring tool
48. Continuously
49. Rats!
50. Pigeon's cry
51. Give help to
53. Mine material

86

ACROSS

1. Slant
5. Former GI
8. Entreats
12. Bend
13. Chopper
14. Stink
15. Middle
16. Flight
17. Supporter
18. Leg part
19. Suggest
21. Beckon
23. Composition
27. Moistened
30. Fabric lengths
33. Duo
34. College vine
35. Pigpens
36. Genesis ship
37. Puppy's bite
38. Plains tent
39. Bar staple
40. Hand warmer
42. Golf instructor
44. Wrathful
47. Beat
51. Loch ——
54. Coffee container
55. Good-natured
56. Vicinity
57. Foot digit
58. Anytime
59. Bikini tops
60. Puzzling
61. Cubicle item

DOWN

1. Support
2. Hard metal
3. Farmer's measure
4. Gloss
5. Endorse
6. Large test
7. Sub, for one
8. Mule's sounds
9. Snaky fish
10. Hair cream
11. Cloud's place
20. Lower
22. Pearl's place
24. Asterisk
25. Cockeyed
26. Oxen team
27. Part of a bird
28. No good
29. Misprint
31. Split
32. Intensified
41. Travelers' needs
43. Conceded
45. Car
46. Stepped on
48. Bees' place
49. Glazes
50. Brew coffee
51. Catch
52. Misstate
53. Bering ——

87

ACROSS

1. Startled
5. Mover's vehicle
8. Scorch
12. Sheltered nook
13. Winter hazard
14. Cowboy's gear
15. Hard work
16. Elaborate
18. ___ of Riley
20. Feats
21. Pantry find
23. Lazy person
26. False statement
27. Gawk at
28. Conceited
32. Yellow-pages fillers
33. Celebrations
35. One or more
36. Sloppy condition
38. Nocturnal insect
39. Cup edge
40. Grow choppers
42. ___ a boy!
43. Dote on
46. Garden of ___
48. Confuse
51. Certain horse hair
54. Come ashore
55. Yes, to Popeye
56. Admired star
57. You're something ___!
58. Flower site
59. Period of time

DOWN

1. Ham it up
2. Flirt with
3. Wickedness
4. Cold-cut shop
5. Computer entertainment: 2 wds.
6. Maven
7. High-wire precaution
8. Weepers
9. Cavity
10. Parodied
11. Crimson and carmine
17. Summer cooler
19. Whip
21. Chowder mollusk
22. Helper
24. Distribute
25. Tarred and ___
29. Tenderizing sauce
30. Department
31. Workout locales
34. Remove
37. Take in ___
41. Snakelike fish
43. Competent
44. Distribute, as cards
45. Holds
47. Send out
49. Finger-paint
50. Organ of vision
52. Neither's conjunction
53. Shade tree

88

ACROSS

1. Lime drinks
5. —— drum
9. Overly
12. Certain soft drink
13. Wreck
14. In addition
15. "Empty ——"
16. Achieved
18. Build
20. Offspring
21. Wanderer
23. Fewest
27. Monarchs
31. Pigeon sound
32. Combined, as funds
33. Musical dramas
36. —— a girl!
37. Alpine singers
39. Facial feature
42. Manuscript leaf
43. Dimensions
45. Dispose of
49. Dampens
53. Vehicle for hire
54. —— up to (admit)
55. Willow or birch
56. Kiln, e.g.
57. Bear's home
58. Time long past
59. Musical symbol

DOWN

1. Teenager's woe
2. Activist
3. Alternative word
4. Small carrying bag
5. Bikini piece
6. Writer
7. Position
8. Slow-moving creature
9. Get sun
10. "—— Life to Live"
11. Puzzling
17. Fury
19. Snatched violently
22. Trunk
24. Land division
25. Float aloft
26. Hurl
27. Long poem
28. Nocturnal insect
29. Sit for a picture
30. Baking ——
34. Dowels
35. Voter
38. First baseball game
40. Superman's chest letter
41. Poker pot
44. Zilch
46. Babble
47. Chopping tools
48. Ice-cream measure
49. Stylish
50. Be in debt
51. Country hotel
52. "—— How She Runs"

89

ACROSS

1. Aspen lift: hyph.
5. Solicit
8. Warbled
12. Curved support
13. Floor cover
14. On a voyage
15. Spicy
16. Misjudge
17. "___ Start All Over Again"
18. Tramps
20. Letter before tee
22. Dissolves
24. Hidden supply
28. Venomous snake
30. Luau greeting
32. "The ___ Up There"
33. Vacation hot spot
34. Male voice
35. Descend Mt. Snow
36. Family
37. Courtroom event
38. Envision
39. Method
41. Crinkly cloth
43. Irritate
45. Hardy
48. Certain cereal
51. Glance
53. Leaf opening
54. Regulation
55. Sal, for example
56. Reason
57. Prayer closer
58. Stars' site
59. Evergreen shrubs

DOWN

1. Coal products
2. Bart Simpson, e.g.
3. Escort
4. Verse
5. Grappler
6. "___ Town" (play)
7. Fairy-tale heavy
8. Mexican sauce
9. Operate
10. Tennis divider
11. Car fuel
19. Serving tray
21. Bright red
23. ___ boom
25. One-dish meal
26. Trek
27. Canal of song
28. Invites
29. Sputter
31. Huskily
40. Napkin material
42. Small dog
44. Drums
46. Sketched
47. Affirmatives
48. Bikini top
49. Island liquor
50. Pub drink
52. Gab

90

ACROSS

1. Light fog
5. Had been
8. Load cargo
12. Alpine repeat
13. Tatter
14. Appeared
15. Beef, e.g.
16. Anger
17. Mastered
18. Strangest
20. Hosiery
22. Mimicked
24. Citrus cooler
26. Gusto
27. Conditions
31. Oxidation
33. Nibble
35. Transaction
36. Theme
38. Decrepit horse
40. Whatever
41. Blueprints
44. Sickly
47. Holds tightly
50. Provoke
51. Volcanic dust
53. Preserve
54. Individuals
55. Date frequently
56. Field of study
57. Barber's shout
58. Feeling low
59. Sobbed

DOWN

1. Office note
2. Cooled
3. Most questionable
4. Tribe symbol
5. Inscribed
6. Atmosphere
7. Tired
8. Burned
9. Mexican meal
10. Foretoken
11. Joins
19. Little drink
21. Up to now
23. Acting like
24. Tentacle
25. Twosome
28. Make confident
29. Fellow
30. Cunning
32. Least messy
34. Thirsty
37. Evergreen
39. Miss
42. Pile up
43. Tropical bird
44. Certain golf club
45. Baseball side
46. Work a muscle
48. Get ready
49. Subway scarcity
52. Caribbean or Coral

91

ACROSS

1. Swimsuit part
4. Sail pole
8. Batters
12. Rower's blade
13. Choice word
14. Touched ground
15. Basketball site
16. Mispronounce
17. Zero
18. Gawk
20. "The Blue ——"
22. Wrong
24. Drink heartily
26. To's mate
27. Intense
28. Command to a canine
30. Probability
31. Cheerless
32. Resounding sound
36. Distressed cry
38. Journey
39. That fellow's
42. Quick look
44. Spur on
45. Provoke
47. Small devils
49. Formula
50. So long, to a Brit: 2 wds.
52. Conjunction
55. Fenway ——
56. They go baa
57. Sticky mess
58. Has obligations
59. Brood's home
60. Coop product

DOWN

1. Marsh
2. Beam of light
3. With a protective covering
4. Market
5. Layers
6. Horse's relative
7. Answered
8. Resounded
9. Unsociable
10. Of small importance
11. Office writer
19. —— Rose Lee
21. Era
22. Stir
23. Married
25. Large aquatic mammal
29. Ease off: 2 wds.
31. Add sugar to
33. Boutonniere's kin
34. Cuddle
35. Mine extract
37. Make a choice
39. African animal, for short
40. Related by marriage: hyph.
41. Terrify
43. Flying toys
46. Pens' fluids
48. Ship feature
51. Fearful admiration
53. Holiday drink
54. Collie or poodle

92

ACROSS

1. Periodical, shortly
4. Fizzy water
8. Arched ceiling
12. Slippery
13. Heavy metal
14. Ended
15. Insisted
17. Approach
18. Exercise
19. Picnic visitors
20. Huck Finn's boat
23. Respond
27. Snowhouse
29. Distance traveled
33. Podded vegetable
34. Veiled lady
36. Ailing
37. Win by a nose: 2 wds.
39. Marketplace
41. Feeling
43. Cereal grasses
44. Hit sharply
47. Monkey
49. Concert solo
50. Emphasizes
55. Chap
56. Greases
57. European mountain
58. Gambler's bet
59. Prime
60. Fabric layer

DOWN

1. Halfway
2. Head of a suit
3. Phys ed classroom
4. Moral transgressions
5. General's command
6. Jane or John
7. Also
8. Give
9. Food cooker
10. Protein source
11. Makes mistakes
16. Sedan, e.g.
20. Fully matured
21. Grew older
22. Old Glory
24. Discharges
25. Help
26. Musical notation
28. Clarinet's kin
30. Well-ventilated
31. Type of adhesive
32. Stately trees
35. Sprint
38. Manor
40. Valuable rocks
42. English noblemen
44. Tale
45. Little bird
46. "___ That a Shame"
48. Annoying person
50. Shed tears
51. Bind
52. Maple juice
53. Addition shape
54. Catch sight of

93

ACROSS

1. New York athlete
4. "Wish ___ a Star"
8. Mislaid
12. Ill temper
13. A few
14. Skillful
15. Arm adornment
17. Lower digits
18. Kind of exam
19. Covering
20. Venomous serpents
23. Gather in
25. Boar's home
26. Eating plans
28. Binds
30. Scribble
32. "___ Weapon 4"
36. Shafts of light
38. Curtain
39. Cut wood
42. Hollow stalk
44. Ancient
45. Alert
47. Military
49. Find pleasing
50. Nice
54. Snoozing
55. Stern
56. Talk fondly
57. Flintstones' pet
58. Bettor's numbers
59. Give one's all

DOWN

1. Triangular sail
2. Do wrong
3. English brew
4. ___-friendly
5. Arctic
6. Brunch dish
7. Hair holder
8. Thin strip
9. Woodwind instruments
10. Winter forecast
11. Touchy
16. Fellow leading performer
19. Exceed the limit
20. Promos
21. Attack!
22. As ___ your request
24. Have a cold
27. Multitude
29. Wanders away
31. Oven-cleaner chemical
33. Witch
34. Monkey's cousin
35. Ushered
37. Fastened tightly
39. Light dish
40. Legal excuse
41. Arouse
43. Fear greatly
46. Change over
48. Earth's neighbor
50. Supportive
51. "Sister ___"
52. Neither's mate
53. Squirt gun, e.g.

94

ACROSS

1. Wary
4. At another place
8. Gets tangled
12. Heartache
13. Shrill barks
14. Whitish gem
15. "___ by Myself"
16. Blunders
17. Refute
18. Printed mistake
20. Honking fowl
22. Ironed fold
24. Child
27. Get rid of
30. Torment
32. Contribution
33. Brown in butter
34. Commence
35. Burn
37. Cable news channel
38. Harmonize
40. Horse's sound
41. Row of stitches
45. Burglar's target
48. Toy for windy days
50. Pair
51. Place for a jeans patch
52. Not odd
53. "___ Not Unusual"
54. News flash
55. Geek
56. Kindergartner

DOWN

1. Smack
2. Pious
3. Shrill bark
4. Needle part
5. Bigger
6. Extend out
7. Dangerous curves
8. Method
9. Chimpanzee, e.g.
10. Shade of brown
11. Shady
19. Take place
21. Spring or summer
23. Wicker material
24. Earsplitting
25. Poker payment
26. Clothing colorer
27. Deep-___ pie
28. Global: abbr.
29. Reach across
31. Storm winds
35. Endeavor
36. Grumble
39. Subway coin
40. Look to be
42. Rewrite
43. Limo, e.g.
44. Lion's share
45. Take to the slopes
46. Hill-building insect
47. Payment
49. Finale

95

ACROSS

1. Nights before
5. More, in Mexico
8. Blue spring flower
12. Sow's sound
13. Heidi's mountain
14. Pleasant
15. Part of NFL
17. Large amount
18. Foxier
19. Tot tenders
21. Dish carrier
23. No-win situation
24. "My __ Sal"
26. Gave permission to
28. Vaults
32. Barnyard females
34. Bolt's mate
36. Desperate
37. Doc
39. Lapse
41. Ship deserter
42. Parking field
44. Hoodwink
46. More precipitous
50. Plant again
53. Psalm
54. Dinner hour
56. Long narrative
57. Omelet maker
58. Lemon and orange drinks
59. Be overly fond
60. Endeavor
61. Extended credit

DOWN

1. Billions of years
2. Glass vessel
3. Qualified
4. Tommy Moe, e.g.
5. Male person
6. Regretful word
7. Tear apart
8. Alternatively
9. Agitate
10. Froster
11. Darns
16. Not written
20. "__ the season . . ."
22. Longing
24. Diamond, e.g.
25. Amaze
27. Yank
29. __ chat (informal talk)
30. Distinctive period
31. Studio decor
33. Complete quiet
35. Young boy
38. Law officer
40. Knitting stitch
43. Attract
45. Flower feature
46. Storage building
47. Memo error
48. Spew out
49. Behind
51. Future sign
52. Sundown direction
55. Some

96

ACROSS

1. Vampire, at times
4. Boring instrument
7. Rot
12. "Bells —— Ringing"
13. That woman
14. Dote on
15. Arrived at
17. Hues
18. Hit hard
19. White herons
21. Narrow back street
23. Operate
26. Dishonor
29. Paint-the-town color
31. Riot crowd
32. Friend by mail: 2 wds.
34. Excellent
36. Circle part
37. Lively spirits
39. Small vehicles
40. Foot digit
41. Giraffes' features
43. More melancholy
46. Not bad: hyph.
50. Bind again
52. Aged, as cheese
54. Eat away at
55. Long, skinny fish
56. Third letter
57. Got along
58. Waterless
59. Hazardous curve

DOWN

1. Fishhook point
2. Neighborhood
3. Afternoon events
4. Fire remains
5. Bicycle part
6. Record book
7. Social appointment
8. Fix copy
9. Buyer
10. Sculpture or music, e.g.
11. Approval word
16. Victor, for short
20. Cereal grains
22. Ballerina's jump
24. Classify
25. Decreases
26. Squabble
27. Main character
28. Forefather, e.g.
30. Quacker
33. Allow to borrow
35. Old hat
38. Stared intently
42. Weeper
44. Military employee
45. Feat
47. Formerly
48. Watches
49. Certain poems
50. Game official, for short
51. Noteworthy period
53. Fabric layer

97

ACROSS

1. Coffeehouse
5. Go downhill
8. Ripoff
12. Greasy
13. ___ and caboodle
14. Lullaby
15. Navy or azure
16. Know the ___ and outs
17. Liberal ___
18. Aria
20. Fairies
21. Cold-weather treat
24. Cabbage's cousin
25. Rental unit
28. Watering hole
31. Mother, in Paris
32. Malt liquor
33. Mexican entree
34. Last word
35. Fund-raisers: 2 wds.
37. Hat's edge
39. Beat
40. Concerning
42. Graceful bird
44. Slant
45. "___ Done Him Wrong"
46. Small flaps
50. Fruit pastry
51. Mom's partner
52. Freeway sign
53. Evens' opposites
54. Up to this time
55. Refuse

DOWN

1. Corn on the ___
2. Be troubled
3. Winter illness
4. Unpleasant sight
5. Hide
6. Monarch
7. "___ a Wonderful Life"
8. Delay
9. Breaking pitch: 2 wds.
10. Chip in chips
11. Clutter
19. Feed-bag grain
20. Have a meal
21. Attended
22. Undo
23. Stiff paper
24. Place for a jeans patch
26. Title of respect
27. Forest creature
29. Perfect serves
30. "Second Hand ___"
33. Teased
35. Drilling tool
36. Mountain resort
38. Littlest ones of the litter
40. Singing voice
41. Rosary component
42. Clog, e.g.
43. Cried
45. Enemy agent
47. Wood chopper
48. Vegetable holder
49. Pig abode

98

ACROSS

1. Sheet
5. Restful resort
8. Secret plan
12. Chalet part
13. Decorative vase
14. Jack rabbit
15. Send
17. Beasts of burden
18. Pie piece
19. Venison or pork
21. Malicious look
23. Fixed a shoe
27. Swimsuit top
29. On —— (tense)
32. Climbing vine
33. Tease
34. String instrument
35. Admission charge
36. House shape
37. "—— the Night"
38. Blunder
39. Sheds tears
41. No ifs, ands, or ——
44. Rough file
47. Fragment
50. Skirt length
53. Manipulate
55. Battery fluid
56. Three minus two
57. Waitperson's handout
58. Class
59. Fetch
60. Teenage dance

DOWN

1. Permits
2. Nobleman
3. Accessible
4. Fight with swords
5. Amount of money
6. Demure
7. Contribute to the pot
8. Snapshot
9. Careless
10. Prospector's find
11. Finger count
16. Visit
20. On a cruise
22. Horse strap
24. Rescuer
25. Happily —— after
26. Colorist
27. Beer
28. Madden
30. Dash's partner
31. Small drop
34. Traveler's permit
40. —— and joy
42. Exercise
43. Pound
45. Los Angeles blight
46. Window unit
48. Gambling town
49. Ringo's instrument
50. Welcome ——
51. Like some winter roads
52. Douse
54. Snare

99

ACROSS

1. Brats
5. Puts on
9. Just released
12. Enrage
13. Ram's coat
14. Wood cutter
15. Wisdom
17. ___ your request
18. Pose, as for a portrait
19. Building addition
20. Old hat
22. Signals
24. Inclined
27. Clamp
28. Twosome
32. Put in order
34. Biceps, e.g.
36. Drive on a runway
37. Coarse sand
39. Gremlin's kin
40. Feel indignant about
42. Unkind
45. Citrus cooler
46. Paving stuff
49. Converse, slangily
50. Attempt
53. Earlier than present
54. Achiever
55. Battery liquid
56. "Three ___ in a tub"
57. Sins
58. Connery role

DOWN

1. Annoys
2. Skirt style
3. Scheme
4. Replace a button
5. Abodes
6. Lots
7. Holiday egg drink
8. Dozed
9. Short rests
10. Former spouses
11. Existed
16. Go!
21. Deadly serpents
23. Memory joggers
24. Uninvited picnicker
25. ___ soup (dense fog)
26. Tariff
29. Tennis point
30. Bedridden
31. Ump's relative
33. Become exhausted
35. Say
38. Library user
41. Avoid capture
42. Study for a test
43. Tantrum
44. Aware of: 2 wds.
46. Tex-Mex fare
47. Related
48. TV's Foxx
51. Neither
52. Folder projection

100

ACROSS

1. Doggone it!
5. Pat
8. Thunderous sound
12. Particle
13. Lubricate
14. Keep the faith
15. Pay phone part
16. Summer refreshment
17. Bakery employee
18. Stored
19. Where whales wallow
20. Most recent
21. Make a choice
23. Theater piece
25. Louisiana marsh
28. Barnyard female
29. "___ a Small World"
32. Pasture mom
33. Certain Northern European
35. Brief snooze
36. Beverage for two
37. That guy
38. Fuming
40. Starfish arms
42. "___ to Joy"
43. Prohibits
45. Chop down
47. Streetcar
51. Garden bloom
52. Devotee
53. Crisp, filled tortilla
54. Eat a meal
55. Exercise
56. Repeated sound
57. Hangs low
58. Guided
59. Antlered animal

DOWN

1. Floppy ___
2. Stage part
3. On the pinnacle
4. Biceps decoration
5. Breakfast food
6. Staff member
7. Satisfied
8. Texas fare
9. Finding
10. Big monkeys
11. Boldly forward
22. Aggressive
24. Work dough
25. Lay odds
26. Great respect
27. Pining
28. Tailor's concern
30. Roofing material
31. Eavesdrop
34. Desirous
39. Snared
41. Burros
42. Had
43. Auction calls
44. Concert solo
46. Leisure
48. Relay, e.g.
49. Throbbing pain
50. Anchor

101

ACROSS

1. Contained
4. Originate
8. Organize
12. Stare at
13. Bubbly beverage
14. Relay ___
15. Briny blue
16. Land force
17. Makes a misstep
18. Wet
20. Picnic carrier
22. Valuable metal
24. Big deal
26. Occurrence
28. Fang
32. Male person
33. Henry and Glenn
35. Flying formation
36. Winter forecast
38. Useful legume
40. Drive away
42. Irritates
43. Tropical fruit
46. Lo-cal's kin
48. Lode deposits
49. Cross
51. Tack on
54. Chop finely
55. Bakery offering
56. Prosecute
57. Tibetan oxen
58. Too
59. Evergreen shrub

DOWN

1. Stags
2. Favorable vote
3. Time limit
4. Scheme
5. Sub's weapon
6. Stately tree
7. Perhaps
8. Immediately
9. Meadow bird
10. Measure of farmland
11. Robin's retreat
19. Commercials, for short
21. Restless
22. Precious ones
23. Fiery stone
25. Poet's product
27. Many times
29. Breakfast request: 2 wds.
30. Furniture wood
31. Coop dwellers
34. Bills
37. Wipes out
39. Chomped
41. Ziti, e.g.
43. Physique
44. Formal solo
45. Tie's location
47. "___ each life . . ."
50. Comrade
52. Owed
53. Dawn's moisture

102

1. Cat
5. Fewer
9. Snitch
12. Poker stake
13. Verbal exam
14. Potato bud
15. Get sleepy
16. The Kingston ——
17. Attorney's charge
18. Perplex
20. Brick house
22. Still
23. Coffee vessel
25. Fruit pulp
28. Discourteous
30. Insignificant
31. Rodeo animals
35. Plea
37. Sentry's word
38. Rabbitlike animal
40. Construct
42. Addition shape
43. Lid
46. Root
48. The things there
50. Saucepan
52. Battery fluid
54. Tale opener
55. Fleecy mama
56. Singe
57. Smell
58. Also
59. Pious
60. Connect the ——

DOWN

1. Sucker
2. Bring together
3. Swagger
4. Look
5. City parcel
6. Short, purposeful trip
7. Recited
8. Sailing boat
9. Hockey official
10. Mariner's yes
11. Casual top
19. Feline sigh
21. Collide
24. Hustle
26. Period of note
27. Moray, e.g.
29. "Duke of ——"
31. That lady
32. Gooey substance
33. Chose by vote
34. Engrave
36. Hit repeatedly
39. Antenna
41. Educate
43. Type of apartment
44. Neckwear
45. Equals
47. Mountain refrain
49. Car part
50. Small vegetable
51. —— up (confess)
53. Lacking moisture

ACROSS

1. Coupes
5. Drama part
8. Hazy image
12. Certain exam
13. ___ close for comfort
14. Slacken
15. Chance happening
17. Copied
18. Topic
19. Scorch
21. Valentine symbol
23. Liabilities
27. Sign of the zodiac
29. Admission price
30. Wilt
31. Football measure
33. Move through the air
35. Wise one
36. Snaky letters
38. Took by the hand
40. Cold and damp
41. Office worker, for short
42. Academy ___
44. Espy
46. Imperial
49. Grade
52. Moniker
54. Freezes
55. Pigeon sound
56. Project
57. Convene
58. Conclusion
59. Gets hitched

DOWN

1. Jacket
2. Overhead curve
3. Thoroughbred
4. Pond scum
5. Had a steak
6. Star cluster
7. Handbag
8. Carriers
9. Lick
10. Put to good ___
11. Blushing color
16. Fall on ___ ears
20. Calculate, in a way
22. TKO caller
24. Trivial Pursuit, e.g.: 2 wds.
25. Caesar's garment
26. Gush out
27. Corrosive liquids
28. Sunrise direction
32. Most thickly populated
34. Certain evergreen
37. Soak up
39. Not bright
43. Refresh
45. "___ Bitten"
47. In the company of
48. Rents
49. Cup edge
50. Head of a suit
51. Ball holder
53. Atlantic fish

ACROSS

1. City air problem
5. Stable baby
9. Had a meal
12. Busy place
13. Still
14. Fish part
15. Bird of ill ___
16. Hated
18. Interval
20. "We ___ the World"
21. Carpenter's tool
22. Kingdoms
26. Hesitated
30. Wilt
31. Supply weapons to
32. Canadian whiskey
34. Winter ill
35. Parisian river
38. Had being
41. Family cars
43. Major-leaguer
44. Tub
45. Happens again
49. Preschool pal
53. Reflex-test joint
54. Sense of hearing
55. Notable times
56. Rewrite
57. Skillful
58. Eyepiece
59. Coal measures

DOWN

1. Look for bargains
2. Silent performer
3. Kaput
4. Pleasant
5. ___ crab
6. Verse type
7. Church table
8. Smirked
9. Rearward, nautically
10. Draw even
11. Off the deep ___
17. Burn
19. Bird that hoots
23. Storage area
24. Burrowing mammal
25. Tater
26. Lip
27. Coatrack
28. Surrounded by
29. Hair tint
33. Put into words
36. Nautical defense branch
37. Nail polish
39. Great fury
40. Light-bulb receptacle
42. Fixed look
46. Remove fasteners from
47. Leash
48. Movie locales
49. Split ___ soup
50. Complete circuit
51. Music or sculpture
52. Dark beige

105

ACROSS

1. Alpine sound
5. ___ Wednesday
8. Voice part
12. Harvest
13. Stick for billiards
14. Voyage
15. Long-snouted animal
17. Zoomed
18. Severe
19. Large bag
21. Shoppers' readings
23. Alternate
27. Cry of woe
30. Feeds, as horses
33. Wood chopper
34. Pro's companion
35. Angels' headgear
36. Scientist's room
37. Decorate with frosting
38. Unsightly
39. Rubies, e.g.
40. Fastening peg
42. Rowing device
44. Large-mouthed fish
47. At liberty
51. Small lump
54. Gain control: 2 wds.
56. Traveled by train
57. ___ of Reason
58. Swerve sharply
59. Impersonated
60. ___ leaf
61. Results

DOWN

1. Historic times
2. Coin
3. Detest
4. Met offerings
5. Perform onstage
6. Beef fat
7. Mighty-deed doer
8. Piece of property
9. Racing circuit
10. Dead heat
11. Antique
16. Also
20. Throw lightly
22. Thick carpet
24. "Gilligan's Island" star
25. Final or midterm
26. Confederate soldiers
27. Etching fluid
28. Cuckoo
29. In an updated way
31. "___ the King's Men"
32. Child's toy: hyph.
35. Polynesian dance
39. Channel
41. Waned
43. Ginger ___
45. Wild guess
46. Lengthy tale
48. Baking box
49. Farmer's spring need
50. Miscalculates
51. Bikini piece
52. Sever
53. Verse type
55. Crucial

106

ACROSS

1. Sis's sibs
5. Word-of-mouth
9. "Me ___ My Shadow"
12. Winter Olympics event
13. Small skin opening
14. "___ to the World"
15. Efficient
16. Taunt
17. Hairy jungle beast
18. Laughing ___
20. Gazed
22. Cash in
25. Toy racer: 2 wds.
29. Cuban dance
33. Trim away excess
34. Manta ___
36. Chair
37. Prayer endings
39. Artist's board
41. Plot
43. Harsh
46. Wander aimlessly
51. Be in debt
52. Life of Riley
55. Nothing but
56. Service expense
57. Without end
58. At the summit
59. What bit Cleopatra
60. Close in space
61. Sulk

DOWN

1. Uninteresting
2. Red stone
3. Flirty look
4. Viewed
5. Select
6. Use oars
7. Meet the day
8. A or B
9. Partly closed
10. Negative reply
11. Changed color
19. Circle section
21. Give pleasure
23. Corn piece
24. Hang loosely
25. Health establishment
26. Flight
27. Gold source
28. Edgy
30. Greeted
31. Casey's club
32. Enjoyed a meal
35. Sweet potato
38. Mesh
40. Dominated
42. Fling
43. Divan, e.g.
44. Meadow mothers
45. Cheney, e.g.
47. Ramble
48. Hooked on
49. Utter failure
50. Kind
53. Body of water
54. Botch things up

107

ACROSS

1. — how!
4. Masters
8. Urge
12. Through
13. Shock
14. Military helper
15. "Tea for —"
16. Having talent
17. Store
18. Cat's sound
20. Cafe, e.g.
22. Feels unwell
24. Egyptian snakes
26. Oaf
28. Soak
29. Forest creature
32. Strike
33. In flames
35. Victory sign
36. Superman's initial
37. Naturally!
38. Govern
40. Toward the rising sun
42. As well
43. Detailed account
47. Make a living
49. Enthusiastic
50. Suspend
52. Popular street name
55. — off (irritated)
56. Alternative word
57. Spy
58. Gets it wrong
59. Cane
60. Tend a baby

DOWN

1. Fitting
2. — Orleans
3. Sprinkles
4. Almost closed
5. Venomous, hooded snake
6. 12th letter
7. More precipitous
8. Finished
9. Church ceremony
10. Skunk feature
11. Moist with morning moisture
19. Function
21. Fall flower
22. Tooth trouble
23. Pupil site
25. Cheese with holes
27. Bill settler
29. Wickedness
30. Voyage segments
31. Game of chance
34. Quill
39. Listening organ
41. Strained
43. Speed
44. At all
45. Marina sight
46. Gambling term
48. Ancient
51. Stout
53. Orchid necklace
54. Came together

108

ACROSS

1. Gulp
5. Dad's mate
8. Like the Sahara
12. Chopin or Walesa
13. Hairy jungle beast
14. Pierce with a drill
15. Call out
16. Affirmative reply
17. Astride a horse
18. "___ Came Jones"
20. Camper's cover
21. Sticky stuff
24. Snakelike swimmers
26. Not illuminated
27. Not wet
28. Buff
31. Tour of duty
32. Grow
34. Sewn edge
35. Road bend
38. Lounged around
39. "True ___" (film)
40. Relative of checkers
41. Burn
44. Clean of markings
46. "Gilligan's Island" star
47. Carpenter's tool
48. Confederates, for short
52. Otherwise
53. Lace
54. Something wicked
55. Twelve inches
56. Likewise
57. Withhold

DOWN

1. Agent 007, e.g.
2. Distress
3. "___ Get You"
4. Jellylike dessert
5. Deli spread
6. Unsealed
7. Scanty
8. Borders on
9. Clothesline
10. Smooth out
11. Fender flaw
19. Note
21. Shove
22. Card-game stake
23. Skinny
25. Song's text
28. Agitate
29. Exploits
30. Cribs
33. Clung
36. Midday nap
37. Exert
39. Shake hands with
41. Skilled cook
42. Angel's hat
43. To boot
45. Startled
49. Abel's mother
50. Container
51. Crafty

109

ACROSS

1. Corn-ear center
4. Take wing
8. Record
12. Hairy jungle beast
13. Sluggish
14. On a voyage
15. KO counter
16. Chick's sound
17. City's smaller cousin
18. Supports
20. Royal
22. Adventure story
23. Basker's desire
24. Shoemaking tool
27. Magic word
30. Wooden peg
31. Stress
34. Hosted
36. Weeding tool
37. Hi-fi system
39. Long period
40. Distinct period
41. Volcanic overflow
45. Albacores
47. Mist
48. Rainbow
50. Good-natured
52. Birthday years
53. Walking aid
54. Trace
55. Gallop
56. Omelet ingredients
57. Orbs
58. Hot drink

DOWN

1. Complains
2. Verdi composition
3. Confuse
4. Small drinks
5. Hymn of praise
6. Makes aware
7. Redundant one
8. Computer fodder
9. Separate
10. Mend
11. Garbage receptacle
19. Father
21. Elf
25. Willie Winkie's size
26. Governed
28. Elevated
29. Opening
31. Female pronoun
32. Also
33. Leasing
35. Pop flavor
38. Without effort
42. Detached
43. Fashion
44. Contest site
46. Employs
47. Victory symbols
48. Cold cubes
49. Torn cloth
51. Actor's signal

110

ACROSS

1. Not fully shut
5. Cut
8. Soft lump
12. Facts and figures
13. Play it by — (improvise)
14. Corporate symbol
15. Changed the color
16. To's companion
17. Gain
18. Colony insect
20. Fastened
22. Took an oath
25. Enamored
26. Hardwood
27. Grouchy
29. Lessen
32. Half of a bikini
33. 24-— gold
34. Pigeon's purr
35. Hog's pad
36. Name
37. Owned
38. Backyard dryer
39. Moved upward
41. Put out
44. Solemn lyric poem
45. Not shut
46. Jogged
48. Drum accompaniment
52. Bird's flapper
53. Frying need
54. Special nights
55. Gambler's wager
56. Interfere
57. Cereal grains

DOWN

1. Say further
2. TV host Leno
3. Grazed
4. Jet tracker
5. Exited
6. Rowboat blade
7. Romantic offer
8. Recipe direction
9. Advance
10. Fairy-tale giant
11. Adhere
19. Cravat
21. Alternatively
22. Blubbers
23. Skin woe
24. Word of agreement
25. Specialty
28. Sky water
29. Repeated sound
30. Feathery stoles
31. Foreshadow
38. Sword thrust
40. — to (mention)
41. Des Moines's site
42. Twirl
43. Posted
44. Nothing but
47. Balloon input
49. Wall-climbing plant
50. Toll
51. Racetrack feature

111

ACROSS

1. Recipe verb
5. What cows chew on
8. Wicked
12. Irresistible
13. Single
14. Pupil's surrounder
15. Sleeping
16. Fruited pastry
17. High-wire precautions
18. Designate
19. Quarterback Aikman
21. Gnome's kin
24. Shrub
28. Orange jam
33. Negative word
34. Winning serve
35. Nobleman
36. More than should be
37. —— you kidding?
38. Superb
40. Olympic award
42. Grain
43. Applied
46. Emend
50. Anxious
53. Lend support to
55. Paella ingredient
56. Highway vehicle
57. Take to the slopes
58. Odd's opposite
59. Held back
60. Hankering
61. June honorees

DOWN

1. Thumb through
2. Oompah horn
3. Detail
4. Convert, as coupons
5. Police officer
6. Module
7. Doe or buck
8. Plastic material
9. Great wrath
10. Fired up
11. Superman's letter
20. Frankly
22. Brands
23. Linen source
25. Poker wager
26. Lunchtime
27. Colt's gait
28. Title of respect
29. Farm measure
30. Woody grass
31. Curve
32. Active person
39. Looked slyly
41. Tax-return inspection
44. "The Big ——"
45. Embankment
47. Opera singer
48. Froze
49. Perfect scores
50. Request
51. Victory sign
52. Gremlin
54. Commotion

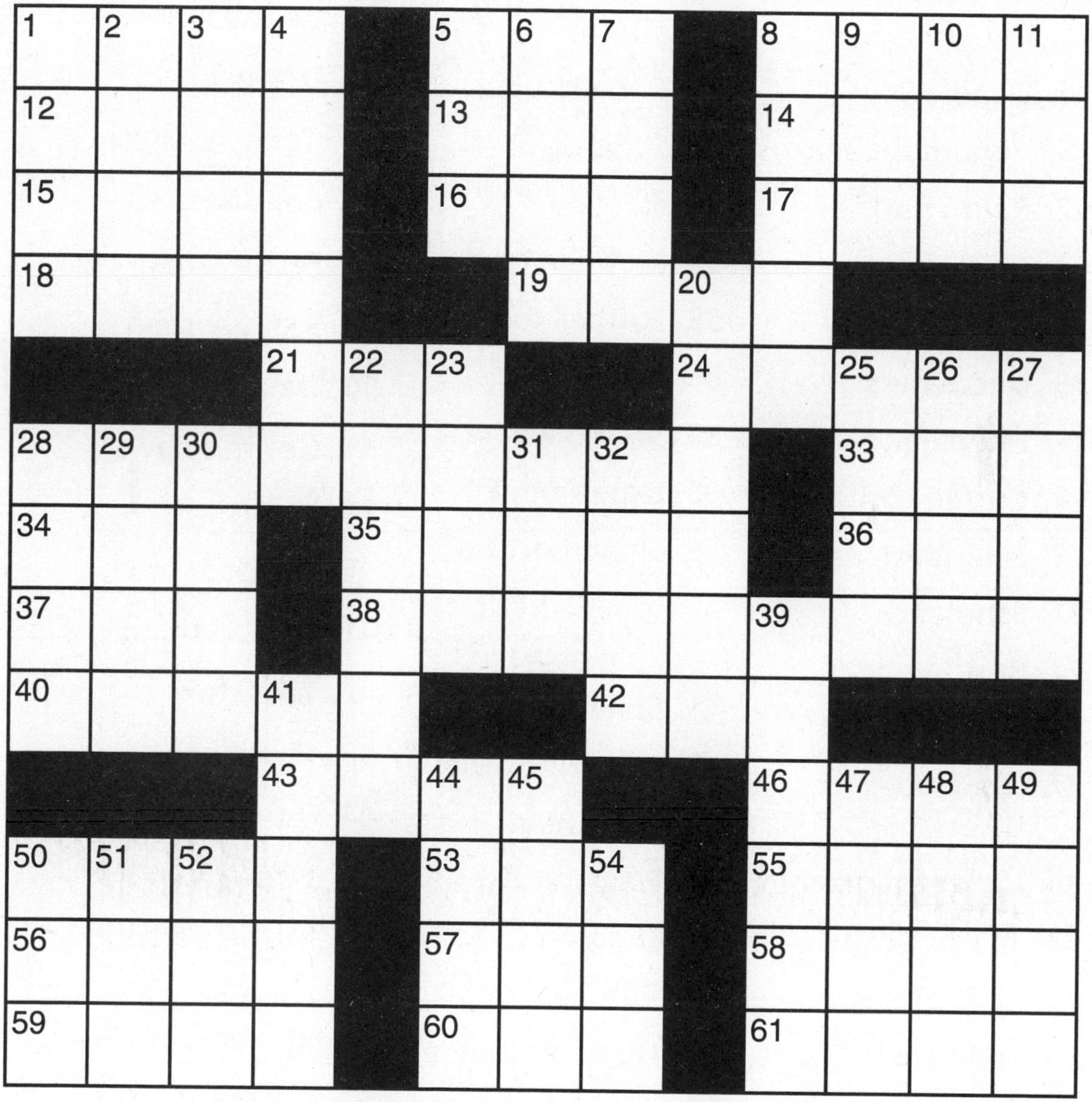

112

ACROSS

1. Cheery
4. Deadlock
8. Venomous snakes
12. Ram's partner
13. Christmas ___ log
14. Hone
15. Decreased
17. Hawaiian dance
18. Coffee container
19. Like sandpaper
21. Scholar
24. Best
26. Heating fuel
27. ___, two, three . . .
28. Ninth follower
32. To's opposite
33. Realtor, e.g.
35. Lode yield
36. Printing errors
38. Might
39. Neptune's realm
40. "Beauty and the ___"
42. Colleague
43. Think constantly about
46. Cooler cubes
48. Slate color
49. Fiercely
54. Metallic fabric
55. Former spouses
56. Spelling ___
57. Stared at
58. Experiment
59. Small portion

DOWN

1. Stylist's goop
2. Fill with wonder
3. Positively!
4. Hair colorist
5. Jogging
6. Pub beverage
7. Hunk of cheese
8. For some time
9. Open-and-___
10. Animal hide
11. Don't go
16. "A Boy Named ___"
20. Shabby
21. Gentle
22. Drafty
23. Gooey substance
25. Considers
27. Fertile areas
29. Scents organ
30. Oak or elm
31. Get the news
34. Locals
37. Minded
41. Valued thing
42. Tent stake
43. Gawk at
44. Donkey's cry
45. Like
47. Movie personnel
50. Lumberjack's implement
51. Decrease
52. Honolulu garland
53. However

113

ACROSS

1. More ___ than good
5. Currier's partner
9. "___ Framed Roger Rabbit"
12. Neighborhood
13. Muck's partner
14. A long time
15. Scheme
16. Nothing but
17. House shape
18. Go through water
20. Mommy's partner
22. Fitness club
24. Most bizarre
27. Chinese skillet
28. Ruckus
29. Electric swimmers
33. "People ___ Funny"
34. Like a horse
36. None
37. Waitperson's handout
39. Pulled apart
40. Female deer
41. Ship sections
43. "War ___ Peace"
44. Lark
47. Similar
49. Bind
50. Opinion sampling
53. Legendary monster
56. Raises, in poker
57. Religious statue
58. Herbal drinks
59. Clear
60. Wet with morning droplets
61. Humanities

DOWN

1. Contains
2. Rainbow's shape
3. Rouse again
4. Papa's lady
5. Instant
6. Contest
7. Foul up
8. Bulbs
9. Gardener's nemesis
10. Grasp
11. Nothing more than
19. College housing
21. Enjoyed dinner
22. Did the breast-stroke
23. Small opening
25. Giver
26. Unceasingly
30. Put in jeopardy
31. Large cat
32. Santa's ride
35. Office furniture item
38. Employ
42. Moderately warm
44. Confound
45. Smoker's tool
46. Pause
48. Particle
51. Shelley offering
52. Deep
54. Rodent
55. Road bend

114

ACROSS

1. This woman
4. Baltic et al.
8. Endure
12. Was victorious
13. Urban vehicle
14. Afresh
15. Rainbow's shape
16. Metal sources
17. Skirt style
18. Punctual
20. "Cadillac ___"
21. King's title
22. Cow's foot
26. Grabbed a bite
27. Salami vendor
29. Statue material
31. Type of sovereign
33. Intensify
35. Skip
38. Sly as a ___
39. Lip
41. Every one
43. High mountain
44. Chewy candy
46. Slipped
48. Display
50. Additionally
51. Wrenched
52. Christmas tree
53. Apparatus
54. Erupt
55. Parodied
56. Polar sight

DOWN

1. Trades
2. Appalling
3. Theater cry
4. Halt
5. Mars's neighbor
6. Paul Bunyan's tool
7. Brother's sib
8. Flight
9. Zoo resident
10. House of Congress
11. String
19. Riot
23. Signs
24. Rowboat necessity
25. ___ bad to worse
28. Mischief-makers
30. To the point
32. Split ___ soup
33. Small amount
34. Lapse
36. Hunting expedition
37. Pleasing to the eye
38. Goes without food
40. Director Oliver ___
42. Evade
45. Had a debt
47. Dawn's moisture
48. Sauna locale
49. With it

115

ACROSS

1. Overwhelms
5. Turn over
9. Beaver barrier
12. Type
13. Parasites
14. Breakfasted
15. Brave man
16. Telephone employee
18. Bother
20. Attended
21. Luster
24. Exultant joy
27. Deep
28. Woodchuck
33. Big chimp
34. Sweater size
35. Fruity drink
36. Courier
38. Allow
39. Craving
40. Twelve dozen
42. Dull one
45. Change color
46. Activate
50. Remotely
54. Work onstage
55. Strong alkalis
56. Advertising symbol
57. Behold
58. Onionlike plant
59. Join

DOWN

1. Cigar residue
2. Gloom
3. Botch
4. Pebble
5. Whip
6. Spout
7. Bartender's rocks
8. For every
9. Computer fodder
10. Particle
11. Scant
17. Mastered
19. Fisherman
21. Bridge term
22. Expectation
23. Flock females
24. Canyon
25. Olympic sled
26. Vital force
29. Telephoned
30. Aura
31. Sonnets' kin
32. Fetches
37. Fat
41. Empire
42. Prejudice
43. A single time
44. Liturgy
45. Student's furniture
47. Unfavorable
48. Vote for
49. Crossed letter
51. Opponent
52. Grow older
53. Spoil

116

ACROSS

1. Atlas part
4. Hurried
8. Tree part
12. Grease
13. Musical quality
14. Word-of-mouth
15. Citrus refreshment
16. Cincinnati nine
17. Brief letter
18. Brewing vessel
20. ___, sealed, and delivered
22. Response
24. Acting like
27. Put up
32. Cleo's river
33. Equipment
34. Angel's hat
35. Bellowing
37. Expensive fur
38. Angora fabric
40. Sudden
44. Related again
48. Pigeons' cries
49. Sprig
51. Deep sorrow
52. Lazy
53. Leisure
54. "It's ___ or Never"
55. Title
56. Shades
57. Cloud's locale

DOWN

1. Ditch of defense
2. Nurse's ___
3. Urgent request
4. Mighty
5. "Dead ___ Society"
6. Hold one's ___ up
7. Meal finale
8. Extended
9. Curling device
10. Companion
11. Ran together, colorwise
19. Committee
21. Deep anger
23. Measure on a scale
24. One or more
25. Boston cream ___
26. Unwell
28. Blueprint
29. Pick up the ___
30. House addition
31. Legal John or Jane
33. Tightly entangled
36. Sprite
37. Blockades
39. Spring up
40. Corrosive substance
41. Foretell
42. Played part
43. Applied
45. Holds
46. Glance
47. Wet with morning moisture
50. Manner

117

ACROSS

1. Front of the leg
5. Shirt protectors
9. TV notices
12. Solitary
13. Drop
14. Romance
15. Motorcar
16. Spread out
18. Injustices
20. Coloring
21. Chest bone
23. Burden
27. Broad-antlered beast
30. Snakelike swimmer
31. Skiing hill
32. Cargo unit
33. Explode
35. Final letter
36. Haunted-house sound
38. "A Boy Named ___"
39. Snake shape
40. Listen
41. Barnyard mother
42. Week part
45. Thundered
50. Old-movie feature
54. Corrode
55. Deep respect
56. BLT topper
57. Volcanic flow
58. Fourposter
59. "___ So Cold"
60. Daisy part

DOWN

1. Cabbage dish
2. 60-minute period
3. Division preposition
4. Downtown lighting
5. More domineering
6. Naughty child
7. Feathered friend
8. Linger
9. Piercing tool
10. Stag's mate
11. Section of grass
17. Water or oil source
19. From Crete, e.g.
22. Redden
24. Trickle
25. Imitates
26. Poor grades
27. Write with acid
28. Folk legends
29. Lower joint
31. Office worker, for short
34. Hopi villages
37. Says further
43. Sleeve fillers
44. Slangy affirmative
46. Night fliers
47. Lamb or pork
48. Building overhang
49. Liquid measure
50. Arrest
51. Pasture mother
52. Get hitched
53. Needle opening

118

ACROSS

1. Roof feature
5. Deeds
9. Summer fruit cooler
12. Debtor's burden
13. Deli side order
14. Woman's undergarment
15. Hopping insect
16. Mama's spouse
17. "___ It Be Me"
18. Tiny green plants
20. Makes by steeping
22. Caught
25. All right: hyph.
27. News flash
29. Zest
33. Gore et al.
34. Places for valuables
36. Dove call
37. Bamboo shoot
39. Heard
41. Eyeball
43. Skating jumps
44. Mosaic-maker
47. Thrown missile
49. Court
50. October birthstone
52. Deteriorates
56. "___ Impossible"
57. "Eyes ___ Shut"
58. Cozy place
59. Car fuel
60. Minus
61. Car for hire

DOWN

1. Santa's helper
2. Need aspirin
3. Neckline shape
4. Paint
5. Serpents
6. Paid notices: 2 wds.
7. Strike lightly
8. Mops
9. ___-bodied seaman
10. Depicted
11. Uses up
19. Sonnets' kin
21. Decay
22. Aspen lift type: hyph.
23. Guideline
24. Word in a threat
26. Bucks
28. "Walking ___"
30. Complexion woe
31. Carol
32. Eros and Zeus
35. Night sight
38. Fawn's mother
40. Boundary
42. Angry dog's comment
44. Branch offshoot
45. Pinch
46. At a ___ (puzzled)
48. Beerlike drinks
51. Humble ___
53. Feathered stole
54. Spar
55. Go down the slopes

119

ACROSS

1. Long narrative
5. Light-switch position
8. Certain fuel
12. Building annexes
13. Ventilate
14. Congressman's assistant
15. Above
16. Golf peg
17. Oozed
18. Housecoat, e.g.
19. Whirl
21. Gator's cousin
24. Gets closer to
28. Declaration
32. Crop
33. Bother
34. Covered walkway
36. Beer's kin
37. Went up
39. Window material
41. Yes votes
42. "Star Trek II: The Wrath of ___"
44. At that time
48. Black-tie event
51. Deep in pitch
53. Citrus fruit
54. Entity
55. Glimpse
56. Correct
57. Variety
58. Bizarre
59. Establishes

DOWN

1. Burn
2. Female singer
3. Rounded lump
4. Qualities
5. Cookie grain
6. Savage
7. Costing nothing
8. Telegram
9. Grease
10. Summer thirst-quencher
11. ___ Zeppelin
20. Main course
22. Frankfurter condiment
23. Bird of ill ___
25. Cry of sorrow
26. Took a drive
27. Zipped
28. Thick carpet
29. Lofty
30. Voyaging
31. Not one
35. Large dwellings
38. Paddled
40. Slide smoothly along
43. Too
45. Skin
46. Spew out
47. Circus safeguards
48. Destroy the interior of
49. "___ Wednesday"
50. Mouth edge
52. Joined in matrimony

120

ACROSS

1. Den
5. Character
9. Catch 40 winks
12. Unit of farmland
13. Wild duck
14. Ma that baas
15. Encounter
16. Plus
17. Fetch
18. Traveler's stop
20. Drifter
22. Races
25. Patch the roof, again
28. Because
29. Benefit
31. Congressional assistant
32. Plug-in choo-choo: 2 wds.
35. Volcano flow
36. Cold-cuts seller
37. Baby
38. Style
40. Blockades
42. Deficiency
44. Authority
45. Play unit
47. Settles a bill
49. Certain woodwind
53. Female deer
54. Family diagram
55. Ages
56. Grass
57. Barnyard animals
58. Chatters

DOWN

1. Flight
2. Air hero
3. Ill-humor
4. Bind again
5. Normal quality
6. Moray, e.g.
7. Flog
8. Rug site
9. Argue
10. Bewilder
11. Favorite
19. Robin's pad
21. Teddy ——
22. —— system
23. Stopped
24. Heavens
26. Sonora sayonara
27. Charter
28. Hat material
30. Lunar events
33. Flog
34. Level
39. Distance down
41. Sticky
43. Challenge
45. TV announce-ments
46. Dove sound
48. Yearning
50. Bikini part
51. Furniture wood
52. Snakelike curve

121

ACROSS

1. Camel feature
5. Ticket remnant
9. Minor falsehood
12. Given by mouth
13. ___ out (demolish)
14. Be
15. Giant
16. Bland-tasting
18. Postpone
20. Stage signal
21. Belief
23. Length
27. Wring
30. "___ Yeller"
32. Fruit dessert
33. Long period
34. More prone
36. Decorate a cake
37. Picasso's work
38. Perched
39. Pleasure craft
41. City haze
43. Wearing clothes
45. Fore-and-___
47. Washes away
51. Confidential
55. Gather a harvest
56. Admiration
57. Make over again
58. Choice word
59. Marry
60. Sleuth Nancy ___
61. Large number

DOWN

1. Head covering
2. Strong impulse
3. Shopping place
4. Begs
5. Rocked
6. Small container
7. Swanky
8. Wooer
9. Chew the ___ (talk)
10. Hot temper
11. Floral plot
17. Gave permission
19. Very small quantities
22. Slogan
24. Legendary
25. Impersonator Little
26. Tournament
27. Afternoon socials
28. Bait
29. Toward the middle of
31. Washer's companion
35. Associate
40. Worships
42. Common fuel
44. Underneath
46. A president
48. Hollow
49. Life of Riley
50. Spout
51. Handle roughly
52. Female sheep
53. Rosy
54. Juicy thirst-quencher

122

ACROSS

1. Mr. Hanks
4. Athletic side
8. Suits
12. Certain sheep
13. Shaft
14. Alpine sound
15. Moreover
16. Oven
17. Rest against
18. Bearded bloom
20. Coils
22. Brogue
24. Curse
25. Adhere
26. Distress
27. Corn spike
30. Diatribe
31. Long fish
32. Lion's hair
33. Peeper
34. Ham it up
35. Fox trot, e.g.
36. Not con
37. Heed
38. Unobserved
41. Ontario, e.g.
42. Tree juices
43. Ellipse
45. Snaky curve
48. Fume
49. Marceau, e.g.
50. Pecan, e.g.
51. Sanctums
52. 12 months
53. Agent

DOWN

1. Afternoon beverage
2. Admit
3. Healing potion
4. Removing
5. Have being
6. 100%
7. Cigarette type
8. Cartoon cat
9. Sorbets
10. Not this
11. Male heirs
19. Charter
21. Small
22. Unit of land
23. Brick material
26. Soak
27. Water containers
28. A single time
29. Has-___
31. Low-priced fare
32. Conceal
34. Common verb
35. Caller
36. Vermin
37. Pack animal
38. Employed
39. Dub
40. Revolve
44. Strive
46. Eat late
47. Filthy place

123

ACROSS

1. Songbird
5. Fluid rock
9. Dunk
12. Potential steel
13. Prayer conclusion
14. Color
15. Proven
16. Limit food intake
17. Be mistaken
18. Corroded
20. Power tool
22. Deli loaf
23. Initial for Superman
25. Mexican sauce
28. Solemn vow
30. Servant
31. Kitchen garments
35. Throws out
37. ___ and proper
38. Sandwich
40. ___ down (softened)
42. Cigar's remains
43. TV host Linkletter
46. Show contempt
48. More modern
50. Luau necklace
52. Is unable
54. Better half
55. Coffeepot
56. Uncertain
57. Bright flower
58. Quip
59. Boston ___
60. Golf gadgets

DOWN

1. Metric quart
2. Draw up in order
3. TV's "___ 66"
4. Jeans patch site
5. Junior
6. Surrounded by
7. Swerve
8. Nonsupporters
9. Varnish
10. "___ Gang"
11. Apiece
19. ___ sign
21. Gold-threaded fabric
24. Cloth belt
26. Pose
27. TV airings
29. His and ___
31. Liable
32. ___ and con
33. Washing off
34. Peck film, with "The"
36. Wayne of films
39. Moneymaker
41. Type of coffee
43. Conscious
44. Fasten again
45. Lock of hair
47. Lessen
49. Radiate
50. Tote
51. Notable span
53. Soak up some rays

124

ACROSS

1. Guilty, e.g.
5. TV notices
8. Bullets, for short
12. Disposes of
13. Dove sound
14. ___ one's lips
15. Mimicked
17. Birthday dessert
18. Lodging place
19. Estimates
20. Shrunk
24. Look-alike
27. Gathers
31. Damp
32. Loves excessively
33. Desk wood
34. Confuses
36. Agile
37. Fork or knife
39. Bridal contribution
42. Snooped
46. Biblical sibling
47. Tall, lanky person
50. Angered
51. Large vase
52. Comfort
53. Pay mind to
54. Attempt
55. Went over the limit

DOWN

1. Demure
2. Exec's auto
3. Censor
4. To the back
5. Behave
6. Deer's mother
7. Patch of grass
8. Penny ___
9. Beef or pork
10. Manufacture
11. Poetic works
16. Beerlike beverage
19. Guns the engine
21. Small task
22. Gobbled up
23. ___ rehearsal
24. Duo number
25. Spider's structure
26. "___ a Wonderful Life"
28. Food for dipping
29. Roofing material
30. Upper atmosphere
32. Responsibility
35. Coiled
36. Inclines
38. Bed-and-breakfast
39. Punctuation mark
40. Band instrument
41. "The Way We ___"
43. Bath need
44. You're something ___!
45. Property document
47. Except
48. Botch
49. Some

125

ACROSS

1. Runner's goal, sometimes
5. ___ and letters
9. Type of bean
12. Potent particle
13. Give off fumes
14. Fierce anger
15. Went by bus
16. Solar events
18. Smack
20. Furthermore
21. Certain farmer's locale
23. Thin strip
27. Quick to learn
30. Wood product
32. Need a massage
33. Midday nap
35. More creepy
37. Intend
38. Exploited
40. Society gal
41. Highway vehicle
42. Similar
44. Tripped
47. Converses
51. Fearless
55. Ivy
56. Sword beater
57. English queen
58. Exude
59. Messy abode
60. Recognized
61. City properties

DOWN

1. Musical measures
2. On the summit of
3. Baking ingredient
4. Make right
5. How ___ you?
6. Remember
7. Inform
8. Takes to the slopes
9. Sib
10. Crude metal
11. Affirmative response
17. Arctic or antarctic
19. Held onto
22. Hawaiian feast
24. Corrosive stuff
25. Biblical pronoun
26. Oregano, e.g.
27. Poisonous serpents
28. Stack
29. Sports group
31. Steal a glimpse
34. Make like a bloodhound
36. Splice film
39. Contact-lens solution
43. Bellybutton
45. Geologic periods
46. Highway divider
48. Chauffeured car
49. Make out of yarn
50. Thickens
51. Raises
52. Volleyball barrier
53. Some
54. Bear's burrow

126

ACROSS

1. Maple juice
4. Examine
8. High-school dance
12. Tell a whopper
13. Model T, e.g.
14. Overhanging roof part
15. Lemon cooler
16. Sly gaze
17. Bronze and Iron
18. Fuses
20. Fight site
21. Scoundrel
25. Ravel
28. Stick candy
33. Ready to eat
34. Expert person
35. Bride's headpiece
36. Telephone employee
38. "___ the Lonely"
39. Tidier
41. Thing of value
45. Hosiery fiber
49. Halt, to a horse
50. Had bills
53. Miner's product
54. Parent
55. ___ and aft
56. Caboose, e.g.
57. Gabs
58. Fright
59. Secondhand

DOWN

1. Cabbage salad
2. General's helper
3. Rind
4. Mexican sauce
5. Hint
6. Dined
7. And not
8. Partridge's tree?
9. Latest fashion
10. Broiler
11. Flat hill
19. Laundry machine
20. Fully
22. Schedule
23. Cold-weather treat
24. On one's toes
25. To's mate
26. Split
27. Gorilla, e.g.
29. Creamy white
30. Cattle holder
31. Grease
32. Tissue layer
37. Picnic pest
40. Finisher
41. Cockeyed
42. Former Queens stadium
43. Marinate
44. Organs of hearing
46. Crazy
47. Not written
48. Geek
50. Not at work
51. Anguish
52. Distinctive period

127

ACROSS

1. Box lightly
5. Ride the wind
9. Heartbreaking
12. Yarn
13. Shower-wall material
14. Force open
15. Baghdad's country
16. Last
18. Aftermath
20. United
21. Tiny bits
23. Walrus tooth
27. Not as tall
30. Chef's need
31. Grow fatigued
32. Ump's kin
34. "Lonesome ___"
35. Memorable time
36. Proposed candidate
38. Thaw
40. Festive occasions
41. Rower's paddle
43. Stage shows
47. Preschool pal
51. Magazine stand
52. Electric ___
53. Froster
54. Kind of skirt
55. Had a taco
56. Bear homes
57. Santa's vehicle

DOWN

1. Mix
2. Whittle down
3. Word of regret
4. Need
5. Stammer
6. Furnace fuel
7. Female voices
8. Equine control
9. Restful resort
10. Rembrandt's specialty
11. Tint
17. Ran across
19. Parking place
22. Sporting facility
24. "Wish ___ a Star"
25. Conserve
26. Reflex site
27. Goblet part
28. Engage
29. Exam type
33. Binders
34. Takes weapons from
37. Scratch
39. Doll or kite
40. Elegance
42. In the company of
44. Send
45. Teen trouble
46. Unexpected slide
47. ___ soup (fog)
48. Authorize
49. Pub drink
50. Five and five

128

ACROSS

1. Cabbage salad
5. Declines
9. Deadly snake
12. Carpet's surface
13. Name word
14. Ewe's call
15. Decade part
16. Fast-food order: 2 wds.
17. Possess
18. Ignited again
20. Omens
22. Stately tree
24. Slippery surface
25. Considerably
26. Positive vote
27. Celebration
30. Blush
32. Joined, as metal
36. Quarrels
38. Notable span
39. Nasty child
42. Strike lightly
43. Use a wok
44. Cover again
46. Mode
48. Painting, e.g.
49. Muscle strain
51. Single units
54. Stage hint
55. Meager
56. Cruising
57. Complete
58. Carpenter insects
59. Thick wool

DOWN

1. Agent
2. Stretch out
3. Warned
4. No longer are
5. Tempting
6. Infant's footwear
7. Hidden microphone
8. Conceited person
9. Dwelling
10. Woodcutter
11. Certain flower
19. Type of prisoner
21. Egg-shaped
22. Cock an ___
23. Caustic stuff
28. Cold-weather garments
29. Irritable
31. Computer input
33. Safeguard
34. Bungle
35. "Night and ___"
37. Outcome
39. Support
40. Summer TV fare
41. Performed a role
45. Mama's fellow
47. Take it easy
50. Debate side
52. Wiggly sea creature
53. Took a pew

129

ACROSS

1. Not in
5. Cruiser
9. Each and every
12. Hill's partner
13. Not exciting
14. 20th letter
15. Depicted
16. Deserts
18. Parsley unit
20. Chooses
21. Pitcher spout
24. Narrate again
26. Powerful speaker
28. Pub
32. Buffalo
33. Wireless set
34. Real ___
36. Tornado warnings
37. "Moonlight ___"
39. Blue above us
40. Hit sharply
43. Soiled
45. Dampness
47. Corrupt
51. Vaselike vessel
52. Mine rocks
53. Sales pitch
54. Become
55. Marries
56. Await judgment

DOWN

1. Remark further
2. Armed conflict
3. Pub order
4. Evergreen plants
5. Gazer
6. Custom
7. Mirror reflections
8. Ink holder
9. At the summit of
10. Ash Wednesday to Easter
11. Smaller amount
17. Unit of currency
19. On the double
21. Earring's place
22. Bearded bloom
23. Gone by
25. Cowboy's rope
27. Browns bread
29. Keats wrote them
30. Pig's comment
31. Curious
35. Bear with
36. Anxiety
38. Televised
40. Conceited
41. Had on
42. "___ We Got Fun"
44. Cry
46. Pull or haul
48. Strive
49. Small hotel
50. Went first

1 2 3 4 5 6 7 8 9 10 11
12 13 14
15 16 17
18 19 20
21 22 23 24 25
26 27 28 29 30 31
32 33
34 35 36
37 38 39
40 41 42 43 44
45 46 47 48 49 50
51 52 53
54 55 56

130

ACROSS

1. Took a dip
5. Last letter
8. Question starter
12. Predinner reading
13. Malt beverage
14. Station wagon, e.g.
15. Feed-bag grains
16. ___ your request
17. List entry
18. Excessive desire for wealth
20. Glass container
22. Round object
24. Place for a workout
27. Fortified place
31. Made like a cow
33. Performing on stage
34. Carried
35. Caught
36. Big-game stalkers
37. Tailor's concern
38. South American pack animal
40. Youngster
41. Spicy dish
46. Sandwich mart
49. Paid notices
51. Hollywood's ___ Sandler
52. Spoken
53. Common ailment
54. Undergarment
55. Wire enclosure
56. Longing
57. Towel word

DOWN

1. Haze
2. Corrode
3. Wager
4. Ponder
5. Swat
6. Football side
7. Supernatural
8. Mourn
9. Simple cabin
10. Snacked
11. Male cat
19. Diminish
21. Annual information book
23. Sty dweller
24. Flatfish
25. Look
26. Says further
27. Tub
28. Real-estate measure
29. Plant part
30. Father's Day gift
32. Away from home
34. Sing without words
36. Hilt
39. Covered in foliage
40. Mah-jongg piece
42. Food mixture
43. Dormant
44. Animal's shelter
45. Mischievous ones
46. Sawbones
47. Generation
48. Dally
50. Daystar

131

ACROSS

1. Circle section
4. Daze
8. Permits
12. Additionally
13. Leaf opening
14. Korea's locale
15. Cooperative
17. Beef dish
18. Intern
19. Cover charge
20. Apprise
23. Boxing site
26. Expectorate
29. Unseat
31. Horde
32. Durango fare
33. Bikini top
34. Scoundrel
35. Big chimp
36. Ship part
37. Lazy
38. Jewish title
40. Denomination
42. Gobble down
43. Corrosive substances
47. Gentlemen
49. Coast
52. Spur on
53. Huff and puff
54. Coal weight
55. Muddle
56. Crafts' partner
57. Disposed

DOWN

1. Minute particle
2. Dressing gown
3. Dorm inhabitant
4. Ginger, e.g.
5. Foot end
6. Coffeepot
7. Actual profit
8. Light producer
9. Highly regarded
10. Lace
11. Cut
16. Duplicate
19. Lard
21. Hoop site
22. Entices
24. Carol
25. Competent
26. Leading lady
27. Daddy
28. Polar sights
30. Buyer's attraction
34. Tether
36. Toolbox
39. Army posts
41. Hurls
44. Minute amount
45. Fall
46. Posted
47. Total amount
48. Bad humor
49. Chic getaway
50. Cock an ——
51. Social insect

132

ACROSS

1. As well
4. Mice, to cats
8. Small devils
12. Talk fondly
13. Icicle hanger
14. Folk tales
15. Peace agreements
17. Robber's spoils
18. Disencumbers
19. Transports
20. Attribute
23. Flat-faced dog
24. Fortune
25. Guessed roughly
31. Territory
33. Stir-fry vessel
34. Adore
35. "The Daily Planet," e.g.
38. Hot drink
39. Have a go at
40. Revise
42. Building floor
45. Enormous
47. Judd Hirsch series
48. Inquisitiveness
52. Scored a hole in one
53. Hymn closer
54. Wager
55. Away
56. Ice mass
57. Howl

DOWN

1. Drama part
2. Negative linking word
3. Fawn's mother
4. Tiny
5. Plunder
6. December 24 and 31
7. Correct!
8. Forbidden by law
9. Heavenly body
10. Cattle stick
11. Stage decor
16. "Diamonds —— Forever"
19. Total
20. Arkin of films
21. Aching
22. Hearty meat dish
23. Spear point
26. Persuade
27. Spinning toy
28. Convey
29. Divisible by two
30. The Grateful ——
32. Straddling
36. Force open
37. Violent
41. "All the King's ——"
42. Exclusively male
43. Tortilla snack
44. Yoked beasts
45. Dwelling
46. Patron
48. Grab hold of
49. —— and flow
50. Caribbean or Caspian
51. Porker's pad

133

ACROSS

1. Appear
5. Finds a total
9. Clever
12. ___ the last laugh
13. Old stringed instrument
14. Large snake
15. December 24 and 31, e.g.
16. Lively Scottish dance
17. Chop
18. House of Congress
20. Modifies
22. Toastier
24. Incident
28. Prince of India
32. Paper money
33. Yelp
35. Vatican head
36. Underneath
38. Certain oven
40. Treads heavily
42. Watercraft
45. Picked by preference
50. Bitter anger
51. Too
53. Salesman's model
54. Congressional concern
55. Eye lubricant
56. Fail to mention
57. Snakelike curve
58. Psalm
59. Religious procedure

DOWN

1. "___ So Cold"
2. Roof extension
3. Neck and neck
4. Flat-topped formation
5. Previously
6. Cloth coloring
7. Night vision
8. Retailer
9. Willing's partner
10. Unsatisfactory rating
11. Faucets
19. One plus one
21. Sand ___ (golf hazards)
23. Provide new weapons
24. Taper off
25. Deep-dish dessert
26. Unwell
27. Piggy-bank features
29. Scribble
30. Jungle animal
31. That girl
34. Movie-theater snack
37. Christmas decoration
39. Fire leftover
41. Bowling ___
42. Wicked
43. Historic periods
44. Hems a skirt
46. Stink
47. Big rig
48. Send forth
49. Reminder
52. Yosemite ___

134

ACROSS

1. Let one's —— down
5. Seasonal virus
8. Cry from the nursery
12. Teen affliction
13. Piece of land
14. Woeful expression
15. Temporary shelter
16. Birthday number
17. Petticoat
18. Credit ——
20. Lubricates
21. Intense fear
24. Ditty
26. Baking appliances
27. Repair
28. Paintings, e.g.
31. Shadowy
32. Coldly
34. In addition
35. Bullfight call
36. Wood for a fireplace
37. Geography aid
39. BLT topper
41. Came closer
42. Basins
44. Stretching the truth
46. Mine rocks
47. Timespan
48. Correct copy
52. Grimm monster
53. Solar system's center
54. Govern
55. Experiment
56. Endeavor
57. Lone

DOWN

1. Stetson, e.g.
2. One-spot card
3. Roadside lodging
4. Come back
5. Style
6. Advertising symbol
7. Tool
8. Stoneworker
9. Swamp dweller
10. Send
11. Deadly snakes
19. Curiously
21. Hubbub: hyph.
22. No good
23. Keeps in mind
25. Air part
27. Often-dried fruit
29. Evening garment
30. Having foot digits
33. Most chilly
38. Some beers
40. Valued thing
41. Simpleton
42. Honk
43. Compulsion
45. Thy, updated
49. Couple
50. Not well
51. Letter after ess

135

ACROSS

1. Suggestive
5. Short letter
9. Flood boat
12. Fairy-tale beast
13. Cut down
14. Get the point
15. ___ code
16. Brain
17. Forage grass
18. Bering or White
19. Chubby
20. Vatican leader
21. Beat
23. Tallied
25. Hair colorist
26. Baggage handler
27. Internal ___ Service
29. Faucet
31. Car race
34. Empty inside
35. Rob
37. Does better than a "B"
38. Astonishment
40. Fancy resort
41. Can material
42. Long skirt
44. Pinches
45. Gobble up
46. Bothers
47. Raw mineral deposits
48. Crafty
49. Make ready
50. Update

DOWN

1. Oven-cooked meat
2. Gave consent
3. Soft and smooth
4. Word of assent
5. Doll's cry
6. Highway sign
7. Adult boys
8. Unusual
9. Beached
10. Farm machine
11. Typed (in)
19. Precede
20. Powerful
22. Dangers
23. Male child
24. Go by ship
26. Goldfish, e.g.
28. Personal commitment
29. ___ worker
30. Scads
32. Crave
33. Jabbered
34. Despises
36. Rodeo rope
38. Wheel rod
39. Thin bit of smoke
42. Museum handout
43. Diver's necessity
44. Negative connector

1	2	3	4		5	6	7	8		9	10	11
12					13					14		
15					16					17		
18				19					20			
21			22				23	24				
	25					26						
			27		28							
	29	30						31		32	33	
34								35				36
37						38	39			40		
41				42	43				44			
45				46					47			
48				49					50			

136

ACROSS

1. Fitness center
4. Random try
8. Buddy
12. Breeze
13. Vein of ore
14. Leisure
15. Downturn
17. Tinter
18. Weird
19. Old hat
20. ___ in the bucket
23. More timid
26. Ready to be picked
27. Go fast
28. Cut
31. Chilled
32. Rowboat paddle
33. Hazy image
34. Writer's tool
35. Sentence element
36. Behind schedule
37. Electrical units
38. "It Came ___ a Midnight Clear"
39. Baker or Callow
42. Draw
44. Modify text
45. Swizzle sticks
50. Mood
51. Eat like a bird
52. "___ Are There"
53. Coasted
54. Babbles
55. Subside

DOWN

1. Pathetic
2. Filled dessert
3. Curve
4. Snow vehicle
5. Mushroom
6. Magazine spots
7. Honey insect
8. Moth repellent
9. Feeds, as horses
10. Utilizes
11. Scant
16. Lassoed
19. Each
20. Faucet problem
21. Paddy grain
22. Undo
24. Cupid's target
25. Three-foot ruler
28. Hit
29. Vehicle
30. Songbird
33. More glum
35. Finished first
37. Cast a ballot
39. Matched pairs
40. Admired one
41. Skirt length
43. Bothers
45. Agent 007, e.g.
46. Steeped drink
47. Potato bud
48. Filch
49. Pinch hitter

137

ACROSS

1. "___ a Wonderful Life"
4. Market
8. Circle portions
12. Convened
13. ___-Hoop
14. Plane maneuver
15. Average
16. Carmine and ruby, e.g.
17. Having talent
18. Dusks
20. Sewing cord
22. Sedate
24. Study at the last minute
25. Settler's abode
27. Lassie
30. Was in debt
31. Kind of tree
32. Hint for Holmes
33. At wit's ___
34. Savoring
36. Vehicle
37. Rosters
38. Mountainous
41. Exported
42. Spoke
43. Gardening tool
45. Gnome
48. Lazy
49. Outlet
50. Neither fish ___ fowl
51. Sailors' affirmatives
52. Withhold
53. Porky's digs

DOWN

1. Mischievous child
2. All the ___ in China
3. Poured
4. Fragments
5. Tints
6. Antique
7. Deli meat
8. Warning signal
9. Toga
10. Soda choice
11. Went too fast
19. Contended
21. "If I ___ a Hammer"
22. Foot covering
23. Village
24. Violin's cousin
26. Wobbled
27. Sparkles
28. Uncle's wife
29. Table parts
32. Jaw part
34. Scamper
35. Like freezing rain
36. Staff members, e.g.
38. Most populous continent
39. Titled woman
40. Heap
41. Peel
44. Lumberjack's tool
46. Fortune
47. Cook in fat

138

ACROSS

1. Bridge player's goal
5. Bath powder
9. Depressed
12. Cab
13. October's stone
14. Notable period
15. Frosted
16. Narrated
18. Quit, as a job
20. Workout site
21. Scale
23. Hearty soup
27. Toward the rear, nautically
30. Sweet drink
31. Notable period
32. Natural
33. Submarine locater
35. "Murder, ___ Wrote"
36. Singing groups
38. A couple
39. ___ of a gun
40. Cause to go
41. Herringlike fish
42. Consume
44. Zoo employee
49. Jewel in the rough
53. Prima donna
54. Popeye's affirmative
55. Bakery need
56. Bit of info
57. Stockade
58. Sunday seats
59. Canvas cover

DOWN

1. Move slightly
2. Openwork fabric
3. Tomahawks
4. Skirt type
5. Windstorm
6. Mimic
7. Small blunder
8. Sound of a horse's hoof
9. Give permission
10. Crude metal
11. Money roll
17. Scrape
19. Lawn growth
22. Ninth's follower
24. Prepare a salad
25. Sound repetition
26. "___ Will I Be Loved"
27. Handiworks
28. Bus fee
29. One of a pair
31. Wear away
34. Rouses
37. Keats wrote them
41. Kitchen cooker
43. Over
45. Correct copy
46. Flat bread
47. At all
48. Sloping surface
49. Empty space
50. Observe
51. Masculine types
52. Recent

139

ACROSS

1. Talk too much
5. Ease off
8. Motivate
12. Years long past
13. Hive-dwelling insect
14. Approach
15. Carve
16. Breakfast grain
17. Vision starter
18. Personal
20. Omens
21. Beach sport
26. Ooze out
27. Summer drink: 2 wds.
31. Decimal base
32. Gasps for air
34. Uncooked
35. Uninterrupted
37. Kitchen cooker
39. Curious
41. Pricked
44. Fire remains
45. Thin
46. Miles ___ hour
48. Toward the middle of
52. Nurse's helper
53. Unrefined mineral
54. Invade
55. Walk heavily
56. Accepted standard
57. Class

DOWN

1. Adios!
2. Destiny
3. Curve
4. Lo and ___
5. Hard wood
6. Arthur or Pons
7. Stake
8. Not revealed
9. Marsh stalk
10. Strong wind
11. "___ Tu"
19. Shedding tears
20. Consecrates
21. Reject
22. Yoke animals
23. Air-breather's organ
24. Bout
25. Perform a role
28. Jogger's gait
29. Roof projection
30. Dazzled
33. Picnic nuisance
36. Made a pig's noise
38. Casual pullover: hyph.
40. Fewer
41. Sharp blow
42. Follow
43. Remove fasteners from
46. Dad
47. Historical period
49. No
50. Politician O'Neill
51. Verse poem

140

ACROSS

1. Hot spring
4. "Bonanza" role
8. Seed vessels
12. Foil metal
13. A woodwind
14. Wickedness
15. "___ Sir, That's My Baby"
16. Spinners' works
17. Grab
18. Tricky
20. Like most reptiles
22. Flower part
24. Make a call
25. Complains
27. Took the prize
28. Baltic or Caspian
31. Expert
32. Capsize
34. Yellowish brown
35. Wand
36. Toothpaste option
37. Brewing need
39. British noble
40. Skills
41. Church tables
44. Pub missile
46. Courts
47. Glazed
49. Potato bud
52. Only
53. Not all
54. Burglarize
55. Drove too quickly
56. Couples
57. Deli sandwich

DOWN

1. Enclosure for swine
2. Baked fruit dessert
3. Replied
4. Wolf's sound
5. Follow orders
6. Weep
7. Meeting
8. Flower feature
9. Face shape
10. Holland sight
11. Winter toy
19. Little rascal
21. Halloween treat
22. Old wound
23. Tex-Mex fare
24. Live
26. Glucose
28. First-string players
29. Compass direction
30. Hill insects
33. Keep at it
38. Lobe's site
39. Relieved
41. Shoemaking tools
42. Chicago section
43. Sound pitch
44. Dealer's vehicle
45. Summer quenchers
48. Milk producer
50. "I Got ___ Babe"
51. Subside

141

ACROSS

1. Social grace
5. Male deer
9. Agent
12. Wrong
13. Game on a pony
14. Mexican cheer
15. Radar-screen spot
16. Toward the center of
17. Male child
18. MTV watcher
20. Scarves
22. "Chances ——"
24. Diner's choice
26. Christmas singer
28. Secure with rope
32. Sermon topic
33. Rarer than rare
35. Antique instrument
36. The Grateful ——
37. Tuneful
39. Pass by
42. Tick off
43. Little angel
46. Drain
48. Stable food
49. Popular flower
51. Smallest bills
54. Metallic dirt
55. By any possibility
56. Farm unit
57. Joined in matrimony
58. College bigwig
59. Simple

DOWN

1. Dinner check
2. Hole-punching tool
3. Standards
4. Variety
5. Revolving fishing item
6. Coal weight
7. Sacred table
8. Silly bird
9. Not bad: hyph.
10. Story line
11. Yearnings
19. Elongated fish
21. String instrument
22. Mastered
23. Talk wildly
25. Take a hike
27. ——, but wiser
29. Viewers
30. Blend
31. What the ——!
34. Cowboy film
38. Floral wreath
40. Attracted
41. In excess of
43. Army food
44. Carroll's March ——
45. Looked at
47. Ramble
50. Saltwater body
52. Blunder
53. Understand

142

ACROSS

1. Succession
5. Small bit
9. Night bird
12. Native minerals
13. Dummy
14. Flying formation
15. Church furniture
16. Busybodies
18. Spring up
20. Bucks
21. More agile
24. Burglarize
26. Expert, for short
27. Bottle lid
29. All systems go
33. Feel sick
34. Island greeting
36. ___ soup (thick fog)
37. Sniff
39. Child
40. Graceful tree
41. Legendary toymaker
43. Sounds
45. Most numerous chess piece
48. Garnish
50. Instigator
52. Server
56. Debate side
57. Titled lady
58. Appraise
59. Breakfast food
60. Musher's vehicle
61. Public

DOWN

1. Sever
2. Fury
3. Novel
4. School paper
5. Navy officer
6. Foot digits
7. Weirder
8. Trendy
9. Cake baker
10. Existed
11. Subtraction term
17. Earring's site
19. Bring back
21. Health resorts
22. Prudish
23. Cameo
25. Powerful speaker
28. Cauldron
30. Chimpanzees
31. Take out, as text
32. Thanksgiving side dish
35. Esteemed
38. Gave temporarily
42. Deadly
44. Prelim
45. Walk up and down
46. Highly curious
47. Bird's "arm"
49. Arched ceiling
51. Radio breaks
53. Knock sharply
54. Had dinner
55. Japanese money unit

143

ACROSS

1. Kid
4. Orange drinks
8. Noteworthy act
12. Develop
13. Be distressed
14. Low female voice
15. Motoring nuisance: 2 wds.
17. Nile queen, for short
18. Guided trip
19. Foremost
21. Average: hyph.
22. Pup —
23. Right this minute
26. No longer is
28. Contact-lens solution
30. Scatter
33. Gawked
34. Australian animals
36. Energy
37. Up to this point
38. Toward
40. Makes a boo-boo
44. Beginning
45. Big jump
46. Friendly talk
49. Highway shoulder
51. Actress's job
52. Old stringed instrument
53. Rummy game
54. Shrill bark
55. Load cargo
56. "She's —— There"

DOWN

1. Crude boats
2. Icy abode
3. Suitors
4. Fore's mate
5. Floats
6. Ghostly
7. Ship sections
8. Certainty
9. Plumbing joint
10. Took in food
11. As well
16. Mason's tool
20. Actor's platform
23. Dog's nibble
24. Wallet item
25. Joined
27. Be ready for
29. Jacket parts
30. Cloud's location
31. Part of a foot
32. Ship deserter
35. Tangles
36. Idaho product
39. Freshwater fish
41. Ruler's term
42. Wireless set
43. Used money
44. —— on it (hurry)
46. Yell
47. Work on the garden
48. Each and every
50. Dawn droplets

144

ACROSS

1. Nuclear particle
5. Like a skyscraper
9. Female elephant
12. Peace symbol
13. At a loss
14. Tarzan's friend
15. Swordplay
16. George Bernard ___
17. Testing ground
18. "The Wall ___ Journal"
20. Whiffs
22. Cold-cuts store
23. Dried grass
24. Seek to persuade
26. Confronted
28. Fresher
32. "___ We Got Fun"
34. Lamb's father
36. Begone!
37. Shine
39. Poorly lit
41. Picnic nuisance
42. British saloon
44. Denomination
46. Movie house
49. Except
52. Lyric verse
53. Sis's sibs
55. President's office shape
56. Sleepy's roommate
57. Vein of ore
58. Short reminder
59. Deer's kin
60. Closes
61. Make ready

DOWN

1. Does arithmetic
2. Publicize
3. Cooked too long
4. Brawl
5. More appetizing
6. Bonfire residue
7. Fido's tether
8. Police officer
9. Contact
10. October gemstone
11. Spiders' traps
19. Common tree
21. Spud buds
24. Shake to-and-fro
25. Heating fuel
27. Little bit
29. Anything
30. Age
31. Go bad
33. Measuring device
35. Exploits
38. Mutter
40. Misters
43. Red ___ (Snoopy's nemesis)
45. Walk noisily
46. Morse ___
47. Revered person
48. Collar location
50. Equal
51. Pig's dinner
54. Strange

145

ACROSS

1. Reminder
5. Demon
8. Possesses
12. Racetrack shape
13. Pigeon's sound
14. Rider's command
15. Cheap power source
17. Connection
18. Like a fox
19. Infiltrate
21. Golf gadget
22. Marsh
23. Sacrifice
25. Macaroni shape
28. Squeals
31. Without fat
32. Received
33. Apartment fee
34. Gun
36. Pal
37. Not employed
38. Beaver's construction
39. Play division
41. Host King
43. Hurry along
46. Fido's comment
48. Beach
50. Country road
51. North American deer
52. Entity
53. Santa's vehicle
54. Hair tint
55. Clutter

DOWN

1. Cuts, as grass
2. Black-hearted
3. Oodles
4. Opposite of young
5. Cupcake topper
6. Shed
7. Skunk
8. Nocturnal bird
9. Carved
10. Nary a thing
11. Welfare
16. Cat talk
20. Decompose
22. Filleted
24. Play a lute
25. Santa's helper
26. Hawaiian gift
27. Male voice
28. Twain's Sawyer
29. Final part
30. Hog's haven
32. Lubricated
35. Everybody
36. Coves
38. Male duck
39. Hole punchers
40. Fuel mineral
42. Depend
43. "The Twilight ___"
44. Spring bloom
45. Cherished animals
47. Nourished
49. Sing with closed lips

146

ACROSS

1. Unruly child
4. Legend
8. Basin
12. Afternoon meal
13. Loony
14. Dull pain
15. Baby's vehicle
17. At no charge
18. Put to good ___
19. Protect
21. Saloons
24. Window part
25. Mob scenes
27. Pubs
31. Prepare for combat
32. ___ con carne
34. Three strikes
35. Tropical storm
37. Expensive fur
39. Father's sister
40. Sharp cry
41. Guarantee
44. Brief farewell
46. Track
47. Underscores
52. Observance
53. Hammer or wrench
54. Gallery offering
55. Santa's chariot
56. Distressful cry
57. Habitual manner

DOWN

1. "___ Your Move"
2. New York baseballer
3. ___ for the course
4. Angled additions
5. Skier's stick
6. ___ cube
7. Gracious
8. Confuse
9. Farmer's measure
10. That time
11. Give careful attention to
16. Banish
20. Mr. Presley
21. Unruly child
22. Drafty
23. Cavort
24. Be miserly
26. Scrub clean
28. Choir gown
29. Invalid
30. Stairway unit
33. Truthfulness
36. Pulled with force
38. Sailors' yeses
41. Miscalculates
42. Brad or tack
43. Location
44. Eye feature
45. Shout
48. Moreover
49. Noticed
50. Important timespan
51. Porker's place

147

ACROSS

1. Snakelike curve
4. Cut into squares
8. Finger covering
12. Guy's date
13. Untie
14. Pimples
15. Quick looks
17. Watch over
18. Teamster's rig
19. "Swan Lake" costume
21. Tango's need
24. Mistakes
28. Extremely obvious
32. Mysterious
33. Feel poorly
34. Royal domain
36. Lemon quencher
37. Clan emblem
39. Chicken soup additives
41. Expresses scorn
43. Make a stab at
44. Throat sound
46. Views
50. Stable morsels
53. Lease
56. Run away from
57. Cypress or poplar
58. "___ Done It?"
59. Provide food for
60. Stitched
61. This instant

DOWN

1. Hens' products
2. Discount offer
3. Slender
4. Law officer
5. Raises
6. Sugar source
7. Result
8. Mother ___
9. Playing card
10. Tourist lodging
11. Went in front
16. Catcher's catcher
20. Shudder
22. Friendliness
23. "___ of These Nights"
25. Vocal
26. "Magic Carpet ___"
27. Observes
28. Sluggers' sticks
29. "The ___ King"
30. Voice part
31. Hosiery color
35. Parking place
38. Wiped clean
40. Tinter
42. Factions
45. Extra
47. Gape
48. Resound
49. Pack
50. ___-key
51. Bar order
52. Golf gadget
54. Unfamiliar
55. Five and five

148

ACROSS

1. Hurt
5. One plus one
8. Army food
12. Persuade
13. "___ Send Me"
14. Storm
15. Hubbub: hyph.
16. Lobster ___
17. Room additions
18. ___ of the trade
20. Pound or Frost
21. Washbowls
24. Skating-rink surface
26. Create
27. Solemn lyric verse
28. Cached
31. Mediterranean, e.g.
32. Dawdled
34. Summer cooler
35. Dark beige
36. In fashion
37. Chef's attire
39. Stockade
40. Willingly
41. Business note
44. Stand
46. King-topping cards
47. Shoe tip
48. ___ of Riley
52. "___ So Cold"
53. Lend an ___ (listen)
54. Nights before celebrations
55. Lug
56. Dehydrate
57. Bread and whiskey

DOWN

1. Portray
2. Dove's comment
3. Once owned
4. Strange
5. Errors in print
6. Lamb's fabric
7. Exterior
8. Thin pancake
9. Angel's crown
10. Stare rudely at
11. Sundown direction
19. Prompt: 2 wds.
21. Greatest
22. Region
23. Penn of "Colors"
25. Fragrant trees
27. Antique
28. Tortoise's competitor
29. Hero
30. Withhold
33. Charitably given
38. Potato skinner
39. Sheriff's gang
40. Hot-tempered
41. Ship's pole
42. Mountain refrain
43. Join
45. Lion's greeting
49. Trailing plant
50. Toll
51. Superman's chest letter

149

ACROSS

1. Look
5. Winter virus
8. Gooey substance
12. Yoked draft animals
13. Ingest
14. Get hold of
15. Brewed beverage
16. High or low card
17. Kaput
18. On a regular basis
20. Plunged
21. Spicy dish
24. Use a couch
26. Punch spoon
27. Vigor
28. Wood cutter
31. Building section
32. Part of the head
34. "___ to Evening"
35. Cost
36. Finger count
37. Yearned
39. Turn brown
40. ___ your fingers!
41. Miss America's garb
44. Comment
47. Admire
48. Rower's paddle
49. Absent
53. Colored eye-part
54. Island drink
55. Hue
56. Variety
57. Pig's place
58. Finishes

DOWN

1. Lump
2. Wood chopper
3. Final letter
4. Register
5. Accomplishment
6. Doily fabric
7. Tool
8. Phantom
9. Volcanic flow
10. Kitchen hot box
11. ___ up (make lively)
19. Spanish party
21. Musical staff symbol
22. Healthy
23. Out of action
25. Collision
27. Small bus
28. Section of Manhattan
29. Picnic drinks
30. Gets hitched
33. TV faultfinders
38. Make
39. The things here
41. Thin opening
42. Well-ventilated
43. Bypass
45. Tightly drawn
46. West Point team
50. ___ ton soup
51. Addition word
52. Affirmative vote

150

ACROSS

1. ___ town (flee)
5. Window frame
9. Obstacle
12. Geometric figure
13. Spindle
14. Miner's product
15. Coarse file
16. Suggestive glance
17. Sharp point
18. Brewery brew
19. Melt together
20. Luxury
21. Gaily colored bird
23. Central part
25. Gawks
27. Votes against
28. Ceases
30. Guzzle
32. Badge
35. Principal's domain
37. Mistakes
39. "On Your ___"
40. "God's Little ___"
42. Crow's comment
43. Copy
44. Social slight
45. History
46. Hair goo
47. Grimm heavy
48. Scheme
49. Road bend
50. Snug retreat
51. Hankerings

DOWN

1. Bit of fabric
2. Australian animals
3. Interject
4. Verve
5. Greets a general
6. Chopping tools
7. Streamlined
8. That woman
9. Science of plants
10. Comes up
11. Fend off
19. Precede
20. Blackboard cleaner
22. Transmits
24. Total
26. Family member, for short
29. Iced dessert
30. Ranges
31. Steering devices
33. Setting
34. Mythical beast
35. Play platform
36. Actress Hope ___
38. Rocks
41. Mutts
44. Daughter's brother
45. Secret agent

151

ACROSS

1. Heavy stick
5. Eras
9. Cloth shred
12. Pathway
13. Recital piece
14. House shape
15. Assistant
16. Hair-care tool
17. Noshed
18. Immediately!
20. Nobleman
22. Engraver
25. Mellow
29. Glow
33. Across
34. Cow's chew
35. Falling flakes
36. Energetic people
38. Tint again
39. Comfort
41. Ranch animal
44. Idolized
49. Deposit eggs
50. Partially open
53. Dimwit
54. Woodsman's implement
55. Rich deposit
56. Hero's story
57. Center
58. Originate
59. Tennis match parts

DOWN

1. Applaud
2. Lion's place
3. Remove fasteners
4. Existed
5. Broad tie
6. Sticky glop
7. Common tree
8. Wept
9. Behind
10. ___ saxophone
11. Narrow valley
19. Number of fingers
21. Soar
23. Pastry shell
24. Once held
25. Slender stick
26. Building vine
27. Ink stick
28. Take out
30. Additionally
31. Yo-yo, e.g.
32. Woolly mom
34. Dove's noise
37. Ethics
38. Rosy
40. Sultan's wives
41. Close with a bang
42. Drive on a runway
43. Leered
45. Keats wrote them
46. Line
47. Do film splicing
48. Physicians, for short
51. Write down
52. Cooling beverage

152

ACROSS

1. Gave lunch to
4. Hive dweller
7. Leered
12. Astonish
13. Jogged
14. Entire
15. Most uptight
17. Roar
18. Peep
20. Consumed
21. List of choices
24. Borer
26. In the midst of
28. Hot or iced drink
29. Lode's load
32. Sib
33. Divided
35. Dick __ Dyke
36. Hog's place
37. Island garland
38. Edit text
40. Shows boredom
42. Irritates
43. Drive away
46. T-shirt size
48. Bamboo-eating animal
50. Those who avoid something
54. Bent
55. Agree wordlessly
56. Glance
57. Spools
58. Go for it
59. Give permission

DOWN

1. Plump
2. Woolly female
3. Comfortable room
4. Make, as ale
5. Took pressure off
6. Amusement
7. To each his __
8. Fiend
9. Ms. Lane
10. Differently
11. Property document
16. Dazzle
19. Layer
21. Bulk
22. Send forth
23. Too inquisitive
25. Behind schedule
27. Festive occasion
29. Finished
30. Level of responsibility
31. Last parts
34. Church furniture
39. Moderate
40. Sing like the Swiss
41. Enjoy thoroughly
43. Practice boxing
44. Jack rabbit
45. Tale opener
47. Lord's wife
49. Classified notices
51. Shocking fish
52. Whiskey variety
53. Decide upon

153

ACROSS

1. At the center of
5. Upon
9. Storage compartment
12. Tire
13. Toothed wheel
14. ___ in the hole
15. Pork cut
16. Leisure
17. Mend
18. Naval rank
20. Enjoys a sandwich
22. Beauty-pack material
23. Text of a play
26. Disorderly crowd
29. Light blow
31. Glory
32. Fusses
34. Caspian, e.g.
36. Sandwich mart
37. "___ Rae"
39. A pair
41. "___ Sawyer"
42. Baseball misplays
44. Picnic spoiler
46. Fairy-tale baddie
47. Zoo employee
51. Dawn's moisture
53. Still
55. Extra
56. Sailor's consent
57. Overly proud
58. Blueprint
59. ___-and-breakfast
60. Final parts
61. Quiz

DOWN

1. Equal to the task
2. Satellite
3. Showy bloom
4. Jeans fabric
5. Schedules
6. Herbal beverage
7. Caravan stops
8. Give a sermon
9. Baby's basket
10. Frozen dessert
11. Turn over a ___ leaf
19. Destroy the interior of
21. Marched
24. Shirt type
25. Decorate a tree
26. Tresses
27. Scent
28. Took out a loan
30. Animal companion
33. Air pollution
35. Rouses
38. Show up
40. Single
43. Certain car
45. Lure
48. Skier's apparatus
49. Significant timespans
50. Tenant's payment
51. Small portion
52. Peeper
54. Box top

154

ACROSS

1. Sloop feature
5. Duo number
8. Donkey sound
12. Repeat
13. That guy
14. Price
15. Foot-shaped device: 2 wds.
17. Frank
18. Use an axe
19. Empty inside
21. Healed
22. Took a chair
25. Doorway shelter
28. Religious building
30. Jaw part
31. Horse's dinner
32. Chef's instruction
35. Is unable
37. Organ of sight
38. Assault
40. Provoke
41. Ticket
44. Practice boxing
47. Stairway guard
49. Pigsty sound
50. Generation
51. Spindle
52. Circus safeguards
53. Tree fluid
54. Sage

DOWN

1. Interlace
2. Sprain result
3. Exhibition
4. Stocking tip
5. Multitude
6. Manipulate
7. Breakfast fare
8. Facial ridge
9. Hip-hop music
10. Had food
11. Urge
16. Now and ___
20. Work by Shelley
21. Skirt type
22. Bridge
23. Choir member
24. Trial run
25. Land unit
26. Food for Little Miss Muffet
27. Well-mannered
29. Monastery dweller
33. Skillet
34. Engraves
35. Forty winks
36. Passed with flying colors
39. Jeweled headdress
40. Pesters
41. Hired vehicle
42. Is sick
43. Exultation
44. Child
45. Baked dessert
46. Picnic insect
48. Damp and chilly

155

ACROSS

1. Whip
5. Moral crime
8. Baby's snoozing spot
12. Realm
13. Poem
14. Fabled race loser
15. Hive insects
16. Physician, for short
17. Like the Gobi
18. Plant stem
20. Army cafeteria
21. Texas dish
24. Helpful hint
26. White-sale item
27. Fit out
28. Gremlin
31. Biblical craft
32. Blue and yellow result
34. Honolulu garland
35. You bet!
36. Container covering
37. Baby hooter
39. Race in neutral
40. "___ Business"
41. Mobile starter
44. Downspout feeders
47. Voyage
48. Tango requirement
49. Yodeler's feedback
53. Gape
54. Have a muffin
55. Brought to court
56. Nobleman
57. Bread variety
58. Take care of

DOWN

1. Research place
2. How ___ you?
3. Observe
4. Annoy
5. Baking ingredient
6. Hero
7. Cravat
8. Victor
9. Unlikely
10. Purple flower
11. Flower sites
19. Prickling sensation
21. Pottery source
22. "This Gun for ___"
23. Writing liquids
25. Neglect
27. Primary color
28. Evils
29. Submissive
30. Sympathy
33. "Rosie the ___"
38. Most sensible
39. Cowboy, at times
41. On the peak of
42. Spur on
43. Shower-wall piece
45. To another place
46. Ballot
50. Actor's prompt
51. Biddy
52. Not even

156

ACROSS

1. Reveal
5. Firm grasp
9. Mass
12. Certain exam
13. Ornamental fabric
14. Fruit drink
15. Mother
16. Precious stones
18. Chess pieces
20. Angler's throw
21. Sheep sound
24. Biting bug
27. Bravo preceder
28. Breakfast roll
33. Lodging
34. Appear as a ghost
35. Floral wreath
36. Dispatch carrier
38. Close relative
39. Encourage
40. Amid
42. Grimm monster
45. Brief farewell
46. Of navigation
50. Fit
54. House annex
55. "A ___ in Harlem"
56. Fastener
57. "___ Spot Run"
58. Understood
59. Excursion

DOWN

1. Comic Arnold
2. Distinctive time period
3. On the ___
4. Andean animal
5. Secluded valley
6. Female sheep's mate
7. Frost
8. As ___ your request
9. Festive occasion
10. Bookie's concern
11. Good, better, ___
17. Book of the Bible
19. Engraver
21. Hat's edge
22. Bit of dialogue
23. Long timespans
24. Dig out
25. Supreme Court count
26. Off the right path
29. Chimed
30. Plus
31. Store sign
32. High sound
37. Beef fat
41. Intended
42. Bucks
43. Brisk wind
44. ___ of thumb
45. Whistled
47. Provoke
48. Dismiss
49. Develop
51. Soap or candy unit
52. Recline
53. Deer's kin

157

ACROSS

1. Race section
4. Blacken
8. Twitches
12. Strong anger
13. At this location
14. Given by mouth
15. Encountered
16. Irritates
17. "She ___ a Yellow Ribbon"
18. Aromatic herb
20. Basked, as in the sun
22. Blunder
25. Bee's kin
28. Tiny skin opening
29. Mom's partner
32. Female sheep
33. Thrashes
34. Broadcast
35. Morning drops
36. Land division
37. "___ the Lonely"
38. Disposed of
40. Chimp's treat
44. Idolize
48. Slumbering
49. Fasting season
52. Remit funds
53. Happy
54. Sycamore or dogwood
55. Historic period
56. Disappears, as the sun
57. Bored reaction
58. Took by the hand

DOWN

1. Arm or leg
2. Broad expanse
3. Animal companions
4. Mexican dish
5. Personal pronoun
6. Noah's ship
7. Began again
8. Small city
9. Hard metal
10. Consideration
11. Husky's load
19. Mischief-maker
21. Chimpanzees
23. Strong suit
24. Squirrel away
25. Get married
26. Respect
27. Make a blouse
29. Omelet maker
30. Tanker cargo
31. Move with leverage
33. Horse house
37. Offbeat
39. Dined
40. Captures
41. Sound
42. Well-kept
43. Puts two and two together
45. Milky jewel
46. Extreme anger
47. Ogled
50. Division of time
51. Modern

158

ACROSS

1. On the crest
5. Building addition
8. Kind of test
12. Singe
13. Quilter's gathering
14. Luxury auto
15. Submarine sandwich
16. Scottish instrument
18. Keg
20. Incident
21. Released
24. Perfect serve
25. Farm animals
28. Riotous crowd
31. Sharp
32. Prevail
33. Tar
34. Toothpaste option
35. Accepted
37. Public vehicle
38. Consumers
39. Ados
42. Ice-cream measure
44. Talking bird
46. Not employed
50. Informed about: 2 wds.
51. "___ Willie Winkie"
52. Chief
53. Cozy rooms
54. Shady tree
55. Leered

DOWN

1. Bat wood
2. Golf gadget
3. Rowboat need
4. Go ahead
5. Deteriorates
6. Seep
7. Section of a journey
8. Drab green color
9. Primed
10. Congregation's reply
11. ___ and found
17. Bushel part
19. Some are personal
21. Old Glory
22. ___ pudding
23. Cruel
24. Teen blemishes
26. Deuces
27. Furnace fuel
28. Husband or wife
29. Blown or board lead-in
30. Plots
33. Hobby
35. Elephant feature
36. Seek office
37. Wheat and oat husks
39. Potato
40. Record
41. Do a laundry job
42. Banana skin
43. News flash
45. Shepherd's charge
47. Call it a ___
48. ___ detector
49. Off the deep ___

159

ACROSS

1. Overtake
5. Shoemaking tool
8. Music system: hyph.
12. Hunger
13. Orchid necklace
14. Baking box
15. Most grating
17. Bar orders
18. Lark
19. Go very fast
21. Path
23. Rose up against
27. Summer drink: 2 wds.
31. Impel
32. Immediately
33. Aardvark's snack
35. Ump's relative
36. Shoe spike
39. Greenhouse
42. Quicken
44. Ruth's club
45. Furniture wood
47. Chickens, e.g.
51. Better half
54. Abuse
56. In the know: 2 wds.
57. Pipe joint
58. List of dishes
59. Ownership paper
60. Farm pen
61. Zoomed

DOWN

1. Movies, for short
2. On the peak
3. Wound's mark
4. Keen
5. Tavern brew
6. Not east
7. Metric unit
8. Great fear
9. Climbing vine
10. Charge
11. __ and outs
16. Chair, e.g.
20. Help
22. Team cheer
24. Car part
25. Happily __ after
26. Challenge
27. Foot part
28. Soda flavoring
29. Wool providers
30. __ Arbor
34. Bath basin
37. Show up
38. Kind of shirt
40. Flat boat
41. Tempests
43. Titles
46. Highland garb
48. Sob
49. Fixed route
50. Wall component
51. Sludge
52. Jungle animal
53. __ the mark
55. Rocker Stone

160

ACROSS

1. Capricorn's symbol
5. Shack
8. Skillful
12. That hurts!
13. Single
14. Glum
15. Oak, e.g.
16. Sample
17. Move on wheels
18. Ill will
20. Night fliers
21. Ball
24. Notable period
26. Waikiki wreath
27. Metallic rock
29. Said further
33. Dinghy paddle
34. Synthetic textile
36. Lumberman's tool
37. Halloween handout
39. Small fruit
40. Edge
41. Bird call
43. Shed style: hyph.
45. Splotch
48. Wrong
50. Go down the runway
51. Take to court
52. High-flying toy
56. Unfold
57. "___ Now or Never"
58. Always
59. Twinge
60. Group
61. Colorer

DOWN

1. Obtained
2. "___ Town"
3. Get an "A" on
4. Not those
5. Stockings
6. Individual
7. Sioux dwelling
8. Overseas
9. Puff
10. Temporary calm
11. Snaky fishes
19. Quickly
21. Las Vegas machine
22. Bartlett or Anjou
23. Sign on
25. Varies
28. Santa's aide
30. Mend with stitches
31. Movie-theater sign
32. Dealer's car
35. Greasiest
38. Behaving
42. Desert haven
44. Invited
45. Come to a halt
46. "___ Don't Preach"
47. Draft animals
49. Speechless
53. Wall-climbing plant
54. Casual shirt
55. Sin

161

ACROSS

1. Chatter
4. Woodwind
8. Rests
12. Woolly one
13. Study hard
14. Tooth problem
15. Rocker Stone
16. Restaurant
17. Noteworthy achievement
18. Seven-card —
20. Cooks in the oven
22. Theater worker
24. Tresses
25. Clog or sandal
26. Stringed instrument players
30. Writing implement
31. Cloudy
32. Animal companion
33. Feels the heat
35. Dog's woe
36. Not west
37. Prompting
38. Narrow back streets
41. Caution
42. Hideaway
43. Complain
45. Hot beverage
48. Complexion woe
49. Revise text
50. Be incorrect
51. Gardener's purchase
52. Dividers on court
53. Scoundrel

DOWN

1. Affirmative answer
2. Piercing tool
3. Arch need
4. Happen
5. Small nail
6. Clumsy one
7. Green gems
8. African expedition
9. Sherbets
10. "—— Darn Cat!"
11. Puts
19. Sock part
21. Like suntan lotion
22. Poisonous snakes
23. —— the fat (chat)
24. Valentine's Day symbol
26. Rooks, e.g.
27. Wood sliver
28. Juvenile
29. Buck
31. Visit
34. Ogled
35. Sable, e.g.
37. Refusals
38. Expression of regret
39. Frilly trim
40. Border
41. Abide
44. Verse work
46. Historical period
47. Columnist Buchwald

162

ACROSS

1. Sleeping place
4. Disobeyed highway signs
8. Pots' partners
12. Pro vote
13. Confederate
14. Item
15. Outlaw
17. List of activities
18. Fixed route
19. Made like a crow
20. Wander
23. Resort hotel
25. Received a legacy
28. Shoemaker's helper
31. Record keeper
32. Boll ___
34. Door opener
35. Shore
37. As well as
38. Gust
39. Keen
43. Business note
46. Hired vehicle
47. Hearth fuel
51. Pub drinks
52. ___ presentation
53. Publicize
54. Was a passenger on
55. Sleep
56. Soar

DOWN

1. Law student's exam
2. Gawk
3. Animal's burrow
4. History
5. Think ahead
6. Most aged
7. Colorize
8. Cougar
9. Again
10. Supreme Court count
11. Dress-shirt fastener
16. Fudd or Gantry
19. Service academy student
20. Take a chance
21. "___ in a Lifetime"
22. Seaman's shout
24. Church benches
26. Sum up
27. Golf club
28. Hateful
29. Type starter
30. Soared
33. Arm part
36. Look up to
39. Play the leading role
40. Saint's headgear
41. Chopped
42. Grow
44. Periods of time
45. Liquefy
47. Pro
48. Clod
49. Heating fuel
50. Like the Sahara

163

ACROSS

1. Bachelors' homes
5. American Beauty
9. Infomercials
12. Pass over
13. Holiday log
14. Fold
15. Boundary
17. Go wrong
18. Access
19. Hog's home
21. Winery employee
24. Military vessel
28. Synagogue official
32. Saga
33. Cut the grass
35. Well-groomed
36. First performance
38. Booklovers
40. Punched
42. Grate against
45. Entryways
50. Bullring bravo
51. Listen secretly
54. Convent inhabitant
55. Vice
56. Hill's companion
57. Retrieve
58. Pursue
59. Toboggan, e.g.

DOWN

1. Vatican official
2. Minister's word
3. ___-cheap
4. Provoke
5. Pumpernickel ingredient
6. Absent
7. Dozed off
8. More uncanny
9. Malt drinks
10. Thrown missile
11. Agile
16. Legendary story
20. Arizona's ___ Canyon
22. Point a gun
23. Softball, for one
24. Unite in marriage
25. Gorilla or orangutan
26. Tease
27. ___ diver
29. Honey source
30. Soap or candy unit
31. TGIF part
34. Small
37. Wigwams' kin
39. Attaches
41. Say good-bye
42. Elton's offering
43. Helpful hint
44. Sublet
46. Gambler's concern
47. Voiced
48. Theatrical part
49. Hastened
52. Scramble (for)
53. North American deer

164

ACROSS

1. Piece of turf
4. Cut remnant
8. Flip through
12. Great rage
13. Kind of shirt
14. Walk back and forth
15. Affectionately
17. Realm
18. Unusual
19. Catch
21. Hay place
24. The British ——
26. Half a pair
27. Kitty
28. Violin's cousin
32. See ya!
33. Andes animal
35. Lend a hand
36. Surplus
38. Kind of music
39. Cover with frosting
40. Makes a pig's sound
42. Boats like Noah's
43. Sandwich meat
46. Part of a train
48. Demure
49. Drugstore
54. Land measure
55. Left, nautically
56. Take legal action against
57. Tool hut
58. Favorable votes
59. Barnyard female

DOWN

1. Convene
2. Mine material
3. Burrow
4. Went quickly
5. Friendly
6. Entire
7. Kingly
8. Scanty
9. Part of TLC
10. Smashing serves
11. Tidy
16. Spot
20. Tell again briefly
21. Earring's place
22. Black stone
23. Twelve-inch lengths
25. Barren
27. Stake a ——
29. Hideout
30. Wet with the tongue
31. Works by Keats
34. Eye makeup
37. Wandered
41. Cold and damp
42. Upper-body limb
43. Mineral springs
44. Curved structure
45. Former Italian currency
47. Linkletter et al.
50. Gardener's tool
51. Fireplace dust
52. Billiard stick
53. Japanese money unit

165

ACROSS

1. Wineglass feature
5. Deli offerings
9. Had being
12. Molten rock
13. "Star ___"
14. Deer's kin
15. Cutting tools
16. Completely
18. Little finger
20. Recreation spot
21. Limber
23. Scamps
27. Block
30. Baltic or North
31. Best
32. Freezer abundance
33. Of the city
35. "___ Day at a Time"
36. Clean the blackboard
38. Coal receptacle
39. Take to the altar
40. Convey orally
41. Terminate
42. Summer refresher
44. Appeal
49. Wading bird
53. Pop
54. Grain
55. Cut remnant
56. ___ and proper
57. Bread variety
58. Fulfilled, as a promise
59. Stage furnishings

DOWN

1. Hit sharply
2. City vehicle
3. Fairly matched
4. Disguise
5. More sharply inclined
6. Large vase
7. Heavens to ___!
8. Pass over
9. Little
10. The whole amount
11. Blue yonder
17. Surprise attack
19. Publish
22. Synagogue figure
24. Cat sound
25. Glass section
26. Winter toy
27. Reducing regimen
28. Land parcel
29. Supper, e.g.
31. Interior
34. Plane terminal
37. Shut hard
41. Picket ___
43. Circular plate
45. Deadly snakes
46. Long ago
47. Newsroom word
48. Male sheep
49. "Tea ___ Two"
50. Deposit eggs
51. Finished a meal
52. Hole

166

ACROSS

1. Maple-syrup source
4. Cabbage dish
8. Dubs
12. Shoofly —
13. "Spenser: For —"
14. Land measurement
15. A to Z
17. Skinny
18. Mature, as wine
19. Canvas shelter
20. Lively
23. Dipper
27. Mishaps
28. Letter opening
32. Monkey's relative
33. Very dark wood
35. Commitment
36. Person who interferes
38. Reminder
39. Many times
41. Bucks
42. "Gorillas in the —"
45. Liquid gold
47. Red-pencil
48. Continues on
53. Yanked
54. Let up
55. Chop off
56. Snow vehicle
57. Filled with reverence
58. Crucial

DOWN

1. Saratoga Springs, e.g.
2. Feel terrible
3. Vivacity
4. Type of rug
5. Slander
6. "All the Things You —"
7. Not dry
8. Shred
9. Muscle strain
10. Put on a happy face
11. Exported
16. Feeds, as horses
20. Did the breaststroke
21. Vatican official
22. Woodwind
24. Love deeply
25. Animal shelter
26. "Now I — me . . ."
29. Deadlocked
30. Unspecified amount
31. Pairs
33. Santa's helper
34. Place odds
37. Sign on the — line
38. Lawn tunneler
40. Knotted loop
42. New York nine
43. Matinee star
44. Regal form of address
46. Frozen
48. Black-eyed —
49. Not cooked
50. Lodge member
51. Mama deer
52. Eavesdrop

167

ACROSS

1. Moose's kin
4. "___ Alibi"
7. Used a broom
12. Stocking part
13. Malt liquor
14. Groucho's prop
15. Maker
17. Fuming
18. Retained
19. Most numerous chess piece
21. Sports complex
23. Cookie type
27. Split
30. First-class
32. Sharp
33. Swiss call
34. Rips
36. Least
37. Mind
38. Moon period
40. Fence
41. Sprinted
45. Bangor's state
49. Raised flatland
51. Portrayed
52. Cathedral bench
53. Beg
54. Orals
55. ___-upmanship
56. Golf gadget

DOWN

1. Write with acid
2. Folk knowledge
3. Ship bottom
4. Head topper
5. Fled to wed
6. Showed again, on TV
7. Read quickly
8. Succeed
9. Omelet ingredient
10. Duffer's goal
11. "___ to Remember"
16. Conformed
20. Roll of bills
22. Stalk
23. Most sluggish
24. Without clothes
25. Wood splitters
26. Hit repeatedly
27. Cut
28. Tooth problem
29. Clean
31. Observes
35. Fitness facility
36. Disgraced
39. African mammal, for short
40. Cincinnati team
42. Soil additive
43. Relieve
44. Jazz's Ellington
45. Doorway rug
46. High or low card
47. ___ a living!
48. Butterfly catcher's need
50. Wonderment

168

ACROSS

1. Farmer's measure
5. Walking stick
9. Powdery residue
12. At what time?
13. Draft animals
14. Easy as ___ (simple)
15. Deceives
16. Napa and suede
18. Interlace
20. Crossed letter
21. Auto need
22. Crazes
26. Wasted away
31. Volcano's liquid
32. Relieve
33. Yes, to Popeye
34. Flower wreath
35. Associate
37. ___ ho!
40. Ooze out
42. Golf norm
43. Circle segment
45. Garden flowers
49. Roman vehicles
53. Cab
54. Rower's necessity
55. Release
56. Give off
57. Workout place
58. Watch over
59. Hardens

DOWN

1. Hole-punching instruments
2. Dip's companion
3. Lively dance
4. "___ Pulver" (film)
5. Picnic item
6. Chopper
7. ___ as a pin
8. Keyboard key
9. Copy
10. Raleigh's title
11. "___ So Shy"
17. Make better
19. Rascal
23. Glitzy party
24. Anytime
25. Recited
26. Dull and colorless
27. Humorist Rogers
28. Not employed
29. Hurricane's center
30. Hated
36. Calendar coverage
38. Gooey stuff
39. Scribbles
41. Float aimlessly
44. Center
46. All the ___ (nevertheless)
47. Leave
48. Uses a chair
49. Toothed wheel
50. Dried grass
51. Furnish with weapons
52. Five and five

SOLUTIONS

CROSSWORD 1

```
P A L S   A C T S   M O D
U N I T   C O O P   A N Y
S T A R   A B L E   T E E
H E R A L D   D A T A
      P O E M   R I D G E
W A S   O M I T   C O R D
I L L   P I N E D   R I G
F L E E   C O L A   S P Y
E Y E R S   R E S T
      P R O F   G H O S T S
L E I   N E A R   W H O A
O W N   G A L A   E O N S
P E G   S T E M   L O S S
```

CROSSWORD 2

```
A D S   C H A T   A C R E
L A W   A I D E   N E A R
E Y E   S T E M   K E R R
    E V E   P U L S E S
R A T E   A L O N E
A P P E A S E   I T C H Y
F E E   S H A F T   R O E
T R A I T   P R E V I E W
    D I T T O   A N D S
E M P I R E   I N K
B O L O   P O L L   L O W
B L O T   I D O L   E A R
S E W S   D E B S   D R Y
```

CROSSWORD 3

```
C O D S   P I C   D A N E
O V E N   A L L   U P O N
R E S E T T L E   T E N D
D R I E R   S A T I R E S
    G R A B   R E F
O W N   M U M   N U R S E
W H E N   S O P   L E E R
L Y R E S   D O C   W A R
    S U B   P I T A
S O R T E R S   T A R P S
E V I L   A T T E N D E E
L A C E   G O O   G E N T
F L E D   S P Y   O D D S
```

CROSSWORD 4

```
A C E S   A M P   V E T S
W H A T   B O A   O G R E
L O V E   B O Y S C O U T
S W E E T E N   T A M E S
    R A Y   H U L A
N A M E R   B U N   N E W
A R I D   L A M   R I L E
P E N   B O D   D E A L T
    S T O W   S I C
A L T A R   A L G E B R A
D A R I N G L Y   D E A N
E V E N   A I L   E A S T
S A L T   S T Y   D U P E
```

CROSSWORD 5

L	A	M	A	■	H	A	S	H	■	G	E	L
A	C	E	D	■	I	N	T	O	■	O	R	E
C	H	A	R	■	S	T	U	B	B	O	R	N
Y	E	T	I	■	■	N	O	R	■	■	■	■
■	■	F	L	O	A	T	■	A	G	E	S	■
E	M	P	T	I	E	D	■	G	I	V	E	■
G	E	E	■	P	R	O	B	E	■	F	I	X
G	R	A	B	■	■	B	E	A	S	T	L	Y
S	E	L	L	■	L	E	E	R	Y	■	■	■
■	■	A	H	A	■	■	M	U	S	E	■	■
S	E	A	H	O	R	S	E	■	B	R	A	Y
U	R	N	■	E	V	E	R	■	O	G	L	E
M	A	D	■	R	A	T	E	■	L	E	T	S

CROSSWORD 6

A	S	K	S	■	M	A	R	■	A	R	T	S
S	K	I	T	■	O	W	E	■	B	A	I	T
P	I	T	A	■	P	E	P	■	O	G	R	E
■	■	■	B	L	E	S	T	■	D	E	E	M
A	M	B	L	E	D	■	I	C	E	■	■	■
F	I	R	E	S	■	B	L	O	S	S	O	M
A	C	E	■	S	H	E	E	T	■	H	U	E
R	E	D	H	E	A	D	■	T	R	A	C	E
■	■	A	N	Y	■	B	O	U	G	H	T	■
C	Z	A	R	■	R	O	U	N	D	■	■	■
L	O	U	D	■	I	V	Y	■	E	T	C	H
A	N	T	E	■	D	E	E	■	S	H	O	O
N	E	O	N	■	E	R	R	■	T	Y	P	E

CROSSWORD 7

A	R	M	■	P	R	I	M	■	A	L	E	S
P	E	A	■	A	U	T	O	■	B	O	L	T
E	L	M	■	G	I	S	T	■	U	G	L	Y
R	I	B	B	O	N	■	H	O	T	■	■	■
S	T	O	O	D	■	■	U	S	U	A	L	■
■	■	W	A	R	M	E	R	■	P	L	Y	■
A	I	L	S	■	E	A	R	■	I	S	L	E
D	O	E	■	O	V	E	R	D	O	■	■	■
S	N	I	F	F	■	■	I	T	C	H	Y	■
■	■	A	T	E	■	D	E	A	R	I	E	■
D	I	S	K	■	T	W	I	T	■	E	R	A
A	C	H	E	■	C	O	R	E	■	P	E	R
D	E	E	R	■	H	O	E	R	■	E	S	S

CROSSWORD 8

F	A	T	S	■	R	O	T	■	T	W	O	S
R	I	O	T	■	E	K	E	■	R	A	I	L
O	D	O	R	■	P	A	R	■	U	G	L	Y
M	E	N	U	■	L	Y	R	E	S	■	■	■
■	■	C	R	Y	■	A	S	S	O	R	T	■
S	M	O	K	E	■	F	I	T	■	B	O	Y
O	A	R	■	A	R	E	N	A	■	O	A	K
A	X	E	■	P	E	W	■	T	H	E	M	E
K	I	S	S	E	D	■	P	E	A	■	■	■
■	■	P	R	U	D	E	■	P	L	U	G	■
P	E	T	E	■	C	O	N	■	P	I	N	E
O	V	E	N	■	E	O	N	■	E	M	I	T
T	E	N	T	■	D	R	Y	■	N	E	T	S

CROSSWORD 9

```
A R I D   W A S P   V A T
N O N O   A L T O   I R E
N E S T   S T U D   S I R
    T E T H E R   S T A R
E Y E   H E R D   E A S Y
R E A P E R   Y O N
R A D A R       U S U A L
    D E B   A G E N C Y
T B A R   L A S H   S E E
R A G E   A R C T I C
A G O   T R I O   O R E S
Y E N   W E S T   T E A K
S L Y   O D E S   A W R Y
```

CROSSWORD 10

```
A T E   C H A R   A P E S
P O W   H I D E   T R A P
T E E T E R E D   L O S E
      A W E S   R A C E D
A M B L E D   V I S E
T I R E D   W E D   D A D
O N E S   W A X   J U L Y
P E A   F I R   P U R E E
    K N O T   C A R E S S
O F F E R   S I L O
A L A S   R I V E R B E D
R U S T   I R I S   A Y E
S E T S   B E L T   N E W
```

CROSSWORD 11

```
S T A R   S P A T   C A R
T A P E   T O D O   O N E
O M E N   R O O M M A T E
W E S T   E R R   A X E D
      A R T   E S S
I T A L I C S   C H I C K
T O N   P H O T O   L E I
S T Y L E   D O U B L E D
      I N K   F R O
B R I M   O A F   S T A G
L I T E R A T E   S E M I
A T E   A L O E   E L M S
H E M   G A P S   S L O T
```

CROSSWORD 12

```
O P A L   S E A S   B U N
A R I A   T O F U   O R E
T O M B   A N T S   A G E
      O E R   H I R E D
G L A R E   S K I N
R A P   L A T E   K N E W
E K E   C R Y   A Y E
W E S T   R A S P   M E T
    A N E W   L E E R S
I N T R O   D Y E
C A R   T A T A   R O L E
E R E   E X A M   I D E A
R Y E   R E P S   E D I T
```

CROSSWORD 13

```
M I T T   S T A Y   S P A
O V E R   W O R E   T U B
M Y N A   A I M S   A L L
    I M P L Y   E L S E
K O A L A     M A K E R
I N N   R O S T E R
N E T   I D E A L   T O E
    I N D E N T   I R K
A R E N A     E M C E E
D A N K   C R U D E
O D E   S L U R   R I T E
P A M   H A N G   G O A L
T R Y   E D G E   E N D S
```

CROSSWORD 14

```
L A G   A S P S   D A T A
I L L   S W A P   O P E N
F O E   C I T E   S P A T
T E N D E R   A P E R
    U N L I K E   O D D
C A W E D   M U G   V E E
R I O T   S A P   D A L E
A D O   P I G   O I L E D
B E D   A L E R T S
    P O L L   I T C H E D
S H I P   I D L E   O W E
P E L T   E Y E R   P E N
A Y E S   R E D S   E S S
```

CROSSWORD 15

```
T A L C   L A B   D A W N
A R I A   I L L   O B O E
B E E N   V E E   G L O W
    A M I S S   M E S S
U N C L A D   S E A
R O A S T   K E Y   S H Y
G E L   R A I S E   W O E
E L M   O W N   L L A M A
    I N K   D E E P E R
L I D S   W A I T S
I D O L   A F T   S E W S
F L E A   R A T   O R A L
T E R M   D R Y   N A R Y
```

CROSSWORD 16

```
L I A R   C O T S   R O B
A L T O   A R E A   E V E
P L E A   R I N D   D E N
    R A T E D   P O N D
B R A   T O N S I L
R A P   T O T   D U E L S
I C E M A N   R E S C U E
M E D I C   P E A   H A M
    T H R I L L   O U I
E D I T   E R A S E
G U N   W R A P   A C E D
O A K   O U T S   S O L E
S L Y   K N E E   T O M B
```

CROSSWORD 17

```
S L U R   S O N   P L E D
H O S E   E W E   A I D E
A B E D   D E W   G R I N
H E R O   A D S   O A T S
      N U N   M O D
S E V E N   L A S A G N A
I R E   F R A N C   O A F
P R E V I E W   A D O P T
        I T S   F R Y
A L T O   I L L   E O N S
D U A L   D I E   I R O N
D A M E   E K E   N A N A
S U E T   S E T   G L O P
```

CROSSWORD 18

```
B I G   D A F T   L O T S
O D E   O G L E   E M I T
T E N D E R E R   S I L O
H A T E   E A R   S T E P
        E V E   A P E
C O B R A   I C I N E S S
A R E   P A N E L   L E I
W E D L O C K   A S S E T
        E R R   A F T
S M O G   O W N   I R O N
L I M E   B A T H R O B E
A M E N   A R E A   W O W
B E N D   T E S T   S E T
```

CROSSWORD 19

```
S L O P   A D E   A W A Y
T A X I   S O Y   R A R E
A C E S   I C E   C R E W
R E N T E D   L L A M A S
      O N E   A I D
A P P L E   E S T E E M S
I R E   M I G H T   L A P
L O N G I N G   L E F T Y
      R E F   S E X
U N W I S E   T R I C K S
R A I N   R Y E   S O A P
G I L D   N O W   T A L E
E L L S   O N S   S L E W
```

CROSSWORD 20

```
A S P S   L A G   A C T S
N O O K   A G O   S H O O
T O N Y   P E T I T I O N
E N D L E S S   C E L L S
        A Y E   H E R D
S C O R E   S I R   I V E
H U N K   W A D   U S E R
E E L   B E T   O T H E R
      O G L E   E W E
S H O R E   A M E N D E D
L I K E W I S E   S O L E
A R E A   O E R   I S L E
P E R T   N A Y   L E E S
```

CROSSWORD 21

A	R	T	S		R	I	M			S	H	A	H
W	O	O	L		A	N	Y			P	A	L	E
L	O	G	O		I	N	S			A	N	E	W
S	T	A	T	U	S			T	E	N	D		
			R	E	B	E	L			S	P	Y	
A	D	M	A	N			A	R	M	H	O	L	E
L	O	U	D		S	L	Y			A	M	E	N
A	S	S	E	R	T	S			I	D	E	A	S
S	E	T		Y	E	A	S	T					
			A	S	E	A			E	S	C	A	P	E
R	I	C	H		M	O	D			O	P	A	L
E	C	H	O		E	R	A			P	E	N	S
D	E	E	D		D	E	N			E	D	G	E

CROSSWORD 22

A	S	H		F	A	R	E			S	O	L	E
T	O	O		E	X	A	M			P	R	A	Y
O	D	E		L	I	M	P			R	A	K	E
M	A	R	G	I	N			T	O	I	L	E	D
			A	N	G	L	I	N	G				
E	A	G	L	E			L	E	S	S	E	N	S
B	I	O			T	A	D				S	U	P
B	L	O	S	S	O	M			H	A	S	T	Y
			P	H	R	A	S	E	D				
S	T	O	L	E	N			C	A	S	I	N	O
T	A	X	I		A	P	E	R			G	A	B
A	M	E	N			D	E	N	T			O	N	E
G	E	N	T			O	A	T	H			R	A	Y

CROSSWORD 23

S	C	R	A	M		B	A	D		A	C	T
K	O	A	L	A		I	R	E		G	O	O
I	N	P	U	T		S	C	E	N	E	R	Y
			M	E	S	H			A	D	D	S
R	O	B	S		M	O	A	T	S			
A	X	E		C	U	P	B	O	A	R	D	S
R	E	L	O	A	D		S	A	L	O	O	N
E	N	T	A	N	G	L	E	D		B	O	O
			S	T	E	I	N		H	E	R	B
M	I	N	I			S	T	A	Y			
O	N	E	S	H	O	T		B	E	A	N	S
A	T	E		A	W	E		U	N	L	I	T
N	O	D		Y	E	N		T	A	L	L	Y

CROSSWORD 24

A	W	L		C	E	L	L		A	M	M	O
B	E	E		A	L	O	E		P	A	I	D
E	V	E		N	E	C	T	A	R	I	N	E
D	E	R	R	I	C	K		B	O	L	T	S
			A	N	T		T	U	N	A		
S	P	I	C	E		G	O	T		B	R	A
A	R	M	Y		G	E	M		C	L	A	N
G	Y	M		H	U	E		B	L	E	N	D
			A	M	E	N		M	O	I		
A	C	T	O	R		R	E	S	P	O	N	D
S	O	U	V	E	N	I	R	S		V	I	E
P	O	R	E		E	D	G	E		A	C	E
S	P	E	D		W	E	E	D		L	E	D

347

CROSSWORD 25

L	A	Y		T	R	A	P		A	S	E	A
A	G	E		H	E	I	R		M	O	A	N
P	O	S	S	I	B	L	E		B	U	R	T
		O	N	S		S	P	U	R	N	S	
S	H	R	U	G		P	E	A	S			
T	E	A	L		K	E	R	C	H	I	E	F
E	A	R		L	E	A	V	E		C	A	R
P	R	E	M	I	E	R	E		W	E	V	E
		I	M	P	S		C	A	D	E	T	
R	H	I	N	O	S		R	A	N			
E	A	S	T		A	B	U	N	D	A	N	T
V	I	L	E		K	E	N	O		C	O	O
S	L	E	D		E	D	G	E		T	R	Y

CROSSWORD 26

O	W	E	S		C	L	A	D		C	A	R
P	O	R	T		H	E	R	E		A	G	O
T	O	R	O		O	A	K	S		B	I	D
			N	E	O	N	S		M	I	N	E
G	R	A	Y	E	S	T		B	I	N	G	O
O	U	R		R	I	O	T	E	D			
O	B	T	A	I	N		H	A	I	R	D	O
		R	E	G	A	I	N		A	I	D	
S	A	F	E	R		S	N	I	P	P	E	D
H	U	L	A		F	I	N	E	R			
A	T	E		M	A	D	E		I	D	L	E
R	O	E		A	D	E	S		M	E	A	L
E	S	S		P	E	S	T		E	N	D	S

CROSSWORD 27

A	R	M	S		S	T	A	B		T	A	R
N	E	A	T		P	A	I	L		O	D	E
T	I	M	E	T	A	B	L	E		R	O	D
S	N	A	R	E		S	A	L	T			
			E	E	L	S		T	A	I	N	T
D	E	B	O	N	A	I	R		G	L	E	E
A	P	E		S	T	R	A	P		L	O	X
B	I	A	S		H	E	S	I	T	A	N	T
S	C	R	U	B		S	P	A	R			
			S	P	U	D		N	I	N	T	H
A	S	K		S	O	A	P	O	P	E	R	A
L	E	I		E	D	G	E		O	R	A	L
P	E	N		D	O	O	R		D	O	M	E

CROSSWORD 28

S	O	F	A		G	A	S		S	I	T	S
E	P	I	C		R	I	P		A	L	O	E
T	A	L	C		A	D	E		F	L	E	X
S	L	E	E	T	S		C	L	A	S	S	Y
			P	E	P	P	I	E	R			
P	A	S	T	E		R	A	D	I	A	T	E
E	L	K		N	I	L			P	E	R	
A	L	I	A	S	E	S		S	M	E	A	R
			S	H	A	M	P	O	O			
B	A	S	S	E	T		A	N	N	O	Y	S
A	C	N	E		E	L	L		T	R	A	P
C	H	A	R		S	E	E		H	A	L	E
K	E	P	T		T	I	S		S	L	E	W

348

CROSSWORD 29

S	W	A	P	S			L	A	C	E	D
C	A	S	U	A	L		K	I	M	O	N	O
A	G	E	N	D	A		E	M	E	N	D	S
T	E	A		D	R	A	G	O	N			
		V	E	I	L	S		S	H	O	D	
A	L	M	A	N	A	C			A	D	E	
M	O	O	N		T	O	N		S	L	O	W
E	R	R				H	I	S	T	O	R	Y
S	E	E	R		R	O	C	K	Y			
			A	Z	A	L	E	A		E	R	A
A	W	A	K	E	N		S	T	O	L	E	N
L	A	T	E	S	T		T	E	R	M	E	D
E	X	E	R	T				D	E	S	K	S

CROSSWORD 30

A	M	I	D		M	A	R	E		A	N	D
L	O	C	O		I	R	O	N		W	O	O
A	L	E	S		S	C	A	T	T	E	R	S
S	T	R	E	E	T		D	I	E			
			A	R	T		R	E	S	A	W	
N	A	P		T	E	A	K	E	T	T	L	E
U	S	E	D		A	R	E		H	I	T	S
T	E	R	R	I	T	O	R	Y		R	O	T
S	A	T	I	N		T	O	E				
			E	S	S		S	N	A	P	P	Y
S	H	O	R	T	A	G	E		H	A	L	O
P	E	A		E	V	E	N		O	P	A	L
A	R	K		P	E	T	E		Y	A	N	K

CROSSWORD 31

L	U	L	U		F	E	E		L	E	N	S
O	P	E	N		L	A	B		A	S	E	A
B	O	N	D		A	S	B	E	S	T	O	S
E	N	T	R	A	N	T		V	E	I	N	S
			E	L	K		P	E	R	M		
J	E	S	S	E		F	U	N		A	R	C
A	Y	E	S		N	I	P		S	T	A	R
W	E	T		T	O	N		E	N	E	M	Y
			T	H	U	D		G	E	E		
C	O	L	O	N		D	I	L	E	M	M	A
O	P	E	R	A	T	E	D		R	O	A	R
P	A	R	S		O	L	D		E	D	I	T
E	L	S	E		P	L	Y		D	E	N	S

CROSSWORD 32

F	E	U	D	S			C	H	I	R	P
A	R	R	O	W	S		O	R	A	T	O	R
C	A	N	C	A	N		M	U	S	C	L	E
E	S	S		M	A	T	E	S		H	E	P
			S	P	R	I	N	T				
S	T	R	A	Y	E	D				O	I	L
A	W	A	Y		D	I	M		H	U	L	A
T	O	Y				E	A	G	E	R	L	Y
			L	E	S	S	E	N				
W	A	G		A	N	T	S	Y		P	A	Y
A	B	O	A	R	D		E	S	C	A	P	E
S	L	A	C	K	S		D	E	E	P	E	N
P	E	L	T	S				R	E	A	R	S

349

CROSSWORD 33

C	A	W		M	A	T	H		D	E	S	K
O	R	E		A	S	E	A		O	N	C	E
L	E	N	G	T	H	E	N		S	T	A	Y
D	A	T	A			E	N	D		E	R	R	S
			P	U	N			B	I	D	E	
L	I	K	E	N		W	A	D		A	G	E
A	C	E		I	M	A	G	E		T	O	O
P	E	R		T	A	G		A	R	S	O	N
		O	P	E	N		S	L	Y			
M	E	S	A		M	O	P		E	L	M	S
E	V	E	R		A	B	R	A	S	I	O	N
W	I	N	E		D	E	E	D		P	R	O
S	L	E	D		E	Y	E	D		S	E	W

CROSSWORD 34

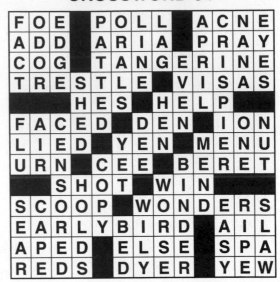

F	O	E		P	O	L	L		A	C	N	E
A	D	D		A	R	I	A		P	R	A	Y
C	O	G		T	A	N	G	E	R	I	N	E
T	R	E	S	T	L	E		V	I	S	A	S
			H	E	S		H	E	L	P		
F	A	C	E	D		D	E	N		I	O	N
L	I	E	D		Y	E	N		M	E	N	U
U	R	N		C	E	E		B	E	R	E	T
		S	H	O	T		W	I	N			
S	C	O	O	P		W	O	N	D	E	R	S
E	A	R	L	Y	B	I	R	D		A	I	L
A	P	E	D		E	L	S	E		S	P	A
R	E	D	S		D	Y	E	R			Y	E	W

CROSSWORD 35

F	O	E	S		O	F	F		P	A	C	T
I	D	L	E		V	I	A		E	C	H	O
R	E	F	E	R	E	E	D		D	E	A	N
			O	N	S		G	A	S	P	S	
G	H	O	S	T		T	O	L	L			
Y	A	N	K		W	A	V	E		A	S	P
M	U	L	I	S	H		E	E	R	I	E	R
S	L	Y		H	O	E	R		A	N	T	E
			R	O	A	D		A	N	T	S	Y
M	A	C	H	O		I	N	N				
A	S	H	Y		O	B	E	D	I	E	N	T
S	E	A	M		A	L	E		T	R	U	E
H	A	R	E		R	E	D		S	A	N	E

CROSSWORD 36

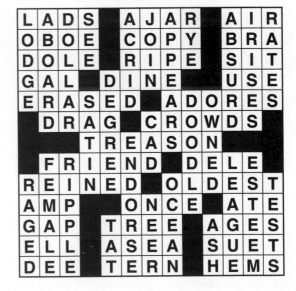

L	A	D	S		A	J	A	R		A	I	R
O	B	O	E		C	O	P	Y		B	R	A
D	O	L	E		R	I	P	E		S	I	T
G	A	L		D	I	N	E		U	S	E
E	R	A	S	E	D		A	D	O	R	E	S
		D	R	A	G		C	R	O	W	D	S
			T	R	E	A	S	O	N			
	F	R	I	E	N	D		D	E	L	E	
R	E	I	N	E	D		O	L	D	E	S	T
A	M	P		O	N	C	E		A	T	E
G	A	P		T	R	E	E		A	G	E	S
E	L	L		A	S	E	A		S	U	E	T
D	E	E		T	E	R	N		H	E	M	S

350

CROSSWORD 37

S	P	U	R		K	I	T		T	R	A	P
W	I	P	E		A	C	E		H	E	R	O
A	T	O	P		Y	E	S		R	A	I	D
M	A	N	E		A	R	T		O	D	D	S
		A	R	K		I	O	W	A			
V	I	S	T	A		F	L	U		B	R	A
A	R	E		B	R	A	Y	S		L	A	D
T	E	N		B	A	R		T	R	E	N	D
	T	R	I	M		A	S	H				
F	L	E	A		P	A	L		Y	A	N	K
L	I	N	K		A	P	T		T	R	E	E
O	N	C	E		G	E	E		H	E	A	P
W	E	E	D		E	R	R		M	A	R	T

CROSSWORD 38

R	O	S	E		A	S	P		S	C	A	M
A	B	L	E		S	P	A		P	O	L	E
S	O	U	L		S	O	Y		R	O	A	M
P	E	R	S	P	I	R	E		A	L	S	O
				A	S	T	R	A	Y			
Z	O	O		S	T	Y		V	E	R	B	S
A	D	U	L	T	S		C	E	R	E	A	L
P	E	T	E	R		T	O	N		F	R	Y
			T	Y	P	I	N	G				
S	L	I	D		A	N	C	E	S	T	O	R
L	O	C	O		U	S	E		W	A	G	E
A	N	E	W		S	E	A		A	C	R	E
T	E	R	N		E	L	L		N	O	E	L

CROSSWORD 39

A	L	A	S		N	O	R		B	O	Y	S
B	I	L	L		A	P	E		I	D	E	A
E	N	L	A	R	G	E	S		Z	E	S	T
D	E	I	T	Y		N	A	N	A			
			G	E	E	K		W	A	R	M	U	P
S	P	A		S	I	S		B	R	I	N	E
E	A	T	S		T	O	O		E	N	D	S
A	R	O	M	A		W	A	S		C	O	T
S	T	R	O	L	L		F	U	M	E		
			L	I	E	D		C	O	M	M	A
S	H	E	D		E	I	G	H	T	E	E	N
L	U	R	E		C	R	Y		H	A	R	E
Y	E	A	R		H	E	M		S	T	E	W

CROSSWORD 40

A	B	L	E		A	L	M	S		S	H	E
R	E	A	R		L	O	A	M		T	E	N
M	A	M	E		G	O	N	E		A	R	T
O	N	E		P	A	N	D	A		P	A	R
R	I	N	S	E			O	R	A	L	L	Y
	E	T	E	R	N	A	L		L	E	D	
			I	M	A	G	I	N	E			
	P	E	N		M	E	N	O	R	A	H	
D	E	L	E	T	E			S	T	R	O	P
E	R	A		U	S	A	G	E		G	A	R
C	U	P		T	A	C	O		L	Y	R	E
A	S	S		O	K	R	A		E	L	S	E
F	E	E		R	E	E	D		T	E	E	N

CROSSWORD 41

```
MINI   SOPS   GAS
ORES   TAUT   UMP
LOWS   URGE   NOR
ENSUED   RISKY
   REV   MINT
ATE   ICER   STOP
ROE   LURKS   AIL
COLA   LIST   SLY
   BUTT   ACT
WIDEN   AGREED
ONE   IDOL   AFAR
OFF   TIDE   MUSE
SOY   ENDS   SLEW
```

CROSSWORD 42

```
ASH   SNAP   TROT
LEI   HOLE   HOBO
LESSENED   IDOL
   ADS   AGREED
SUNG   TOLLS
APE   LOU   OTTER
GOO   APTER   AXE
ANNOY   DRY   KID
   PEKOE   GETS
GOVERN   CRY
IRON   ESTIMATE
GATE   EKES   NOW
SLED   SIDE   DYE
```

CROSSWORD 43

```
CHEF   OPT   MACE
HIVE   RAY   OPAL
AREA   IRK   TERM
TENS   GREAT
   TRIO   LOCAL
ELF   ANT   LEASE
BOOST   ESSES
BURNT   SLY   HAS
STEAL   TASK
   PERRY   NOPE
WISP   AIM   OBEY
ACHE   SPA   WORE
DYED   HEN   NETS
```

CROSSWORD 44

```
ABUT   ASK   ADES
CORE   SON   CURE
TOGA   SUE   HEAT
STEP   ERASE
   OPT   DISARM
TONTO   GEE   TOO
APE   LOADS   ODD
CAR   ICY   TEPEE
OLDEST   RAM
   SHARE   CRAB
SAWS   GAS   EASE
IDEA   ORE   EVEL
BODY   NEE   DEAL
```

CROSSWORD 45

```
ELK FLIT CLUB
SEA EACH HARE
SIN EYER ACNE
  GOT  OBSESS
SLAW AMBLE
TORNADO ARENA
AGO IDLED SON
ROOFS ALERTED
  ALARM AILS
ANGLED  GYM
LOLL OBOE APT
TREE ROAM TEA
OMEN EATS EGG
```

CROSSWORD 46

```
ERR AWAY TEES
VIA CODE AXLE
EMPERORS TIDE
  MIDI EASED
OPTED FLY TRY
NEON STIES
SANDAL ORCHID
  SCORN HIVE
TAD EWE WOMEN
UPEND SHOO
BOLO HAIRLESS
ARTS ILLS LIP
STAY PELT FRY
```

CROSSWORD 47

```
ARK MOPE ACRE
FOE AWAY ROOK
ALE TELESCOPE
RELIT  TAPED
  TEMPTED
AWES ELEMENTS
SOW MOANS OAT
HOEDOWNS AWRY
  INSTEAD
STAGE  IDLED
HONEYBEES EVE
ARTS ORAL TIN
MEET GATE SLY
```

CROSSWORD 48

```
AWAY WEBS DAB
SILO EXIT ICE
SNAG SPRY VIA
  MALTED MEND
TOO AWL EDGY
ADD BASHES
DEEPER ENACTS
  OLDEST HOP
EDEN VIE ANY
ARMY MATRON
GAB SODA GNAT
LIE OPEN REDO
END BEST ELSE
```

CROSSWORD 49

```
S E A   G O L D   L E I
H A N   H O N O R   A P T
E R A   E S S A Y   S I C
      L E S S E N   E T C H
W H Y S   I T E M S
R E S T U P   R E C I T E
A R I A S     N A M E R
P E S T E R   S U P P E R
        E D I C T   E O N S
A C T S   C H I S E L
M A Y   S H A C K   I O N
I N K   P E R K Y   T W O
D E E   A R M Y   E N D
```

CROSSWORD 50

```
H E P   S N I P   T B A R
E A R   T O R E   H E R O
S T O P O V E R   R E E L
        O W E     O P A L
A C N E   L L A M A
R O U T E   A C U T E L Y
C A D   N E S T S   Y E A
S L E E V E S   T W E A K
        N Y L O N   O D D S
T E S T     A D O
H A I R   R E M O D E L S
A C R E   O R E S   L I P
T H E E   W A D E   K E Y
```

CROSSWORD 51

```
G I N   A S P S   S O F T
A C E   T H E E   H A R E
S E W   T O L E R A T E S
      S K I R T   U P S E T
S T R I C T   O L E
H O E D   H O P E   A N D
A T E   S A W E R   B O Y
G E L   T I E R   T R U E
        N O R   A B O U N D
S L I E R   S T A M P
A U T O M A T I C   T A G
G L E N   D A N K   L Y E
E L M S   E G G S   Y E T
```

CROSSWORD 52

```
F A R M S   A S S   S A D
E X E R T   D A M   O R E
N E V E R   D U O   D I E
        I D O L   N O M A D S
S H E   K A R A T E
N O W H E R E   H O S T S
O B E Y   D A D   W H O A
W O R M S   R E A S O N S
        N U T M E G   E S S
T E N S E R   M E L T
A Y E   D I P   N O R M S
C E E   E A R   T R E A T
O D D   S L Y   S E E D Y
```

CROSSWORD 53

T	O	S	S		D	A	M		R	A	T	E
E	D	I	T		I	R	E		U	P	O	N
M	O	L	E		P	E	R		M	E	N	D
P	R	O	P	E	L		E	B	B			
		S	L	O	P		E	A	R	E	D	
A	S	S		A	M	U	S	E		I	V	Y
W	O	E		P	A	R	K	S		C	E	E
L	A	M		S	T	R	E	W		E	R	R
S	P	I	C	E		S	L	A	P			
			A	D	E		E	X	O	T	I	C
L	A	M	B		A	F	T		L	I	M	O
I	D	O	L		C	O	O		A	L	P	S
D	O	M	E		H	E	N		R	E	S	T

CROSSWORD 54

S	P	A	S		S	O	D		I	D	E	A
C	A	M	E		T	A	R		N	E	A	R
A	P	E	D		E	R	A		D	E	S	K
B	A	N	A	N	A		S	W	I	P	E	S
		N	A	M	E	T	A	G				
C	R	I	S	P		D	I	S	O	B	E	Y
O	U	R		P	I	C			A	L	E	
O	N	E	S	H	O	T		M	A	R	K	S
		P	A	R	S	N	I	P				
C	O	H	O	S	T		E	X	P	O	S	E
O	V	E	N		E	W	E		A	K	I	N
P	A	N	G		R	O	D		L	A	R	D
E	L	S	E		S	K	Y		L	Y	E	S

CROSSWORD 55

K	E	P	T		O	F	T		M	A	C	E
I	C	E	R		W	O	O		O	V	A	L
T	H	E	E		E	R	R		O	I	L	S
S	O	L	E	M	N		P	A	D	D	L	E
			U	S	H	E	R					
E	A	S	E	D		A	D	M	I	R	A	L
L	I	E	S		D	U	O		L	O	G	O
F	R	E	S	H	E	N		E	L	B	O	W
			A	L	T	E	R					
S	E	S	A	M	E		M	A	T	T	E	D
A	K	I	N		T	O	P		W	I	P	E
T	E	N	T		E	A	T		I	R	I	S
E	D	G	E		D	R	Y		N	E	C	K

CROSSWORD 56

F	R	O		O	A	K	S		Y	O	G	A
L	A	D		W	I	N	E		E	W	E	S
A	T	E		E	D	E	N		A	N	T	S
B	E	S	T		A	D	E	S				
		H	E	L	D		A	T	L	A	S	
I	N	T	E	R	E	S	T	S		A	G	O
L	A	Y	M	A	N		R	I	S	K	E	D
L	I	P		S	T	A	I	N	L	E	S	S
S	L	O	P	E		L	O	G	O			
		O	R	A	L			T	A	C	T	
B	A	S	K		R	U	N	T		W	O	O
A	C	H	E		C	R	O	W		A	D	O
T	E	E	D		H	E	R	O		Y	E	T

CROSSWORD 57

D	U	M	P		S	A	T		A	W	A	Y
O	R	A	L		E	R	A		P	O	L	E
O	G	L	E		V	E	X		P	O	E	T
R	E	L	A	T	E		I	R	E			
		S	O	N		S	E	A	M	A	N	
A	S	S	E	R	T	S		F	R	A	M	E
P	O	P		P	H	O	N	E		Y	E	W
E	R	A	S	E		P	E	R	S	O	N	S
R	E	S	I	D	E		S	E	W			
		N	O	R		T	E	A	B	A	G	
B	I	N	G		E	Y	E		M	A	K	E
E	V	I	L		C	O	G		P	R	I	M
T	Y	P	E		T	U	G		Y	E	N	S

CROSSWORD 58

L	E	D		S	W	A	T		S	N	O	W
A	P	E		M	O	T	H		T	A	M	E
S	I	C		I	O	T	A		O	V	E	R
S	C	O	W	L		I	N	C	L	I	N	E
		H	E	I	R		L	E	G			
V	E	T	O		D	E	M	O		A	S	P
C	R	E	A	T	E		E	D	I	T	O	R
R	A	N		Y	A	R	N		R	E	L	Y
		T	O	P		A	U	T	O			
S	E	A	F	O	O	D		I	N	T	R	O
P	A	C	T		G	I	S	T		R	A	P
I	S	L	E		R	A	I	L		I	R	E
T	E	E	N		E	L	S	E		M	E	N

CROSSWORD 59

L	I	M	P		M	E	M	O		S	P	A
O	V	A	L		A	W	A	Y		H	O	W
W	E	R	E		K	E	Y	S		A	P	E
		V	A	S	E		T	A	M	E	D	
O	D	E		P	R	O	P	E	L			
M	O	L	D	Y		P	A	R	A	B	L	E
I	D	E	A		G	E	L		R	O	A	D
T	O	D	D	L	E	R		A	M	O	N	G
		D	E	T	A	I	L		B	E	E	
R	E	D	Y	E		T	E	N	T			
E	V	E		W	A	V	E		O	U	T	S
P	I	N		A	T	O	M		O	B	O	E
S	L	Y		Y	E	W	S		K	E	P	T

CROSSWORD 60

O	D	D	S		T	W	O	S		S	P	A
W	E	E	P		U	R	G	E		N	U	N
L	A	C	Y		G	A	L	E		A	R	T
E	R	R		O	P	E	N		T	I	E	
T	E	E	O	F	F		A	C	T	S		
	R	E	N	E	W	A	L		S	H	Y	
		S	E	A	P	O	R	T				
C	E	E		R	E	P	A	I	R	S		
C	O	A	T		S	T	R	E	A	M		
R	U	T		S	E	M	I		V	I	A	
A	G	E		A	X	E	D		D	E	L	I
M	A	R		W	I	N	E		I	R	O	N
P	R	Y		S	T	U	D		M	E	R	E

CROSSWORD 61

```
BUT   SODA  DELE
ONE   TWOS  EVEN
ADS   INCH  SEND
TOTAL      VESTS
    FLIPPER
HEFT  CLATTERS
OAR   PIANO  RAP
PROVINCE  ARMY
    ANGELIC
AMPLE     STACK
DEAL  ODES  VAN
DOPE  LULU  IRE
SWAY  DOME  DEW
```

CROSSWORD 62

```
GLOVE   CRATE
RIPENS  ERASES
ESTEEM  LENSES
WAS   RIFLE
   OGLE   PASTE
DELAYED   HEAL
RAYS  DEB  EELS
ACRE   ROMANCE
THESE  AWED
    VILLA   SPY
SOFTEN  ENTIRE
ONIONS  DEEPEN
BEGOT   RASPS
```

CROSSWORD 63

```
LAP   SUMS  SNOB
OIL   TRIO  PORE
ODE   INDICATED
PEARL  ILL
    ELL   ATLAS
ROWS  EARPHONE
EPIC  FLU  RATE
DEDUCTED   ONES
SNEER   EBB
    OWL   ESSAY
EASYCHAIR   USE
ACHE  ODOR  EEL
TEEN  MYNA  TAP
```

CROSSWORD 64

```
ILLS  IRIS  BIB
MEOW  DUNE  ACE
PIPE  OBSESSED
   ALLY   LESS
PHOTO  COO
ROD   AFTERWARD
OLD  FIEND  CUE
DESPERATE  RIB
   ARM   AGENT
MORN   IDLE
IMITATOR  ATOP
DIP   DATA  RODE
ITS   SNAG  STEP
```

CROSSWORD 65

T	H	I	S		D	O	T	S		C	A	P
H	A	R	T		U	N	I	T		O	W	E
A	L	O	E		S	E	A	R		M	E	N
T	E	N	A	N	T		R	O	A	M		
		M	O	P		A	N	G	E	L	S	
C	R	Y	S	T	A	L		G	E	N	I	E
H	U	E		N	O	G		C	A	W		
A	D	A	P	T		T	A	T	T	E	R	S
P	E	R	I	O	D		M	A	R			
	N	E	A	R		B	R	E	W	E	R	
S	H	E		S	O	I	L		M	O	V	E
P	A	R		T	O	R	E		O	V	E	N
A	D	S		S	P	E	D		R	E	S	T

CROSSWORD 66

P	I	N		B	A	I	L		T	O	T	E
I	R	E		A	L	O	E		Y	A	R	N
T	O	W		L	E	N	T		P	R	O	D
A	N	T	I	S			M	I	S	T	S	
		T	A	M	A	L	E	S				
O	D	E	S		E	L	A	S	T	I	C	S
N	O	R		S	T	A	S	H		C	O	O
S	C	R	A	P	E	R	S		F	E	N	D
		T	U	R	M	O	I	L				
A	R	M	O	R			D	U	S	T	Y	
M	E	A	N		N	O	T	E		P	R	O
M	A	T	E		A	R	I	A		O	U	R
O	P	T	S		P	E	E	L		T	E	E

CROSSWORD 67

S	O	R	T		M	O	D		S	L	I	T
A	P	E	R		O	W	E		T	O	D	O
M	A	M	A		I	L	L		A	B	L	Y
E	L	E	C	T	S		T	E	P	E	E	S
		M	E	A	T	B	A	L	L			
B	I	B		B	E	E		F	E	N	C	E
O	M	E	N		N	I	T		R	E	E	L
A	P	R	I	L		G	O	O		G	E	M
		M	A	T	E	R	N	A	L			
C	R	A	B	B	Y		M	E	D	I	U	M
L	O	L	L		I	C	E		O	G	R	E
O	B	O	E		N	U	N		P	E	G	S
P	E	E	R		G	E	T		T	E	E	S

CROSSWORD 68

D	R	A	G		A	D	O		S	W	A	B
I	O	T	A		C	U	D		H	I	D	E
P	E	E	L		O	N	E	S	I	D	E	D
		L	Y	R	E		T	R	E	S	S	
S	A	T	E	E	N		P	I	T	A		
A	R	R	O	W		A	I	R		W	E	T
N	E	O	N		O	L	E		P	A	V	E
D	A	M		I	L	L		H	I	K	E	S
		B	I	N	D		N	I	C	E	S	T
C	L	O	C	K		K	E	P	T			
H	O	N	E	Y	D	E	W		U	R	N	S
U	S	E	R		O	N	S		R	O	O	K
M	E	S	S		C	O	Y		E	D	G	Y

CROSSWORD 69

A	W	A	Y	■	S	P	A	S	■	H	O	P
S	I	T	E	■	T	I	R	E	■	I	R	E
S	T	E	W	■	O	N	C	E	O	V	E	R
■	■	■	S	T	R	U	T	■	■	P	E	S	T
A	N	T	■	U	M	P	I	R	E	■	■	■
J	U	R	O	R	S	■	C	I	N	E	M	A
A	D	O	P	T	■	■	■	D	E	V	I	L
R	E	T	E	L	L	■	W	I	D	E	N	S
■	■	■	R	E	A	S	O	N	■	R	I	O
A	R	E	A	■	D	I	N	G	Y	■	■	■
L	O	P	S	I	D	E	D	■	E	D	G	E
E	W	E	■	L	I	V	E	■	L	Y	E	S
S	S	E	■	L	E	E	R	■	L	E	T	S

CROSSWORD 70

A	C	E	S	■	G	I	N	■	O	P	T	S
M	A	X	I	■	A	D	O	■	G	O	A	L
I	M	P	S	■	L	E	I	■	R	O	L	E
D	E	E	■	P	L	A	S	T	E	R	E	D
■	■	■	C	A	R	O	L	E	R	■	■	■
L	O	T	I	O	N	S	■	Y	A	C	H	T
O	W	E	D	■	■	■	■	W	H	O	A	■
U	N	D	E	R	■	R	E	P	L	I	E	D
■	■	■	I	C	I	N	E	S	S	■	■	■
F	R	E	I	G	H	T	E	R	■	E	B	B
R	E	A	D	■	O	U	R	■	F	L	E	E
E	A	R	L	■	M	A	G	■	R	E	N	T
E	L	S	E	■	P	L	Y	■	O	D	D	S

CROSSWORD 71

C	H	I	P	■	H	E	R	B	■	S	I	T
R	O	D	E	■	O	R	A	L	■	T	O	E
I	L	L	S	■	M	A	M	A	■	I	T	S
B	E	E	T	L	E	■	■	K	A	R	A	T
■	■	■	O	P	E	N	E	R	■	■	■	■
A	S	H	■	G	L	E	E	■	M	I	S	S
S	P	U	R	■	A	R	C	■	Y	O	K	E
S	A	G	A	■	T	I	E	D	■	N	I	X
■	■	■	C	H	E	E	S	E	■	■	■	■
D	R	A	K	E	■	■	S	N	E	A	K	Y
R	A	N	■	A	S	E	A	■	A	C	N	E
A	R	T	■	P	U	R	R	■	T	H	I	N
T	E	E	■	S	P	R	Y	■	S	E	T	S

CROSSWORD 72

G	R	O	W	■	D	A	Y	S	■	R	Y	E
R	O	D	E	■	A	L	O	E	■	E	O	N
A	D	D	S	■	M	I	K	E	■	C	U	D
D	E	L	T	A	■	G	E	N	I	E	■	■
S	O	Y	■	C	A	N	■	T	I	F	F	■
■	■	■	E	L	S	E	■	E	V	E	R	■
I	N	S	I	D	E	■	R	E	M	E	D	Y
R	A	N	T	■	S	P	R	Y	■	■	■	■
E	P	I	C	■	■	U	S	E	■	S	A	P
■	■	■	C	H	A	R	T	■	D	A	N	C	E
O	A	K	■	T	A	T	A	■	R	A	T	E
A	D	E	■	O	R	E	S	■	C	R	O	P
F	O	R	■	P	E	R	K	■	H	E	R	S

CROSSWORD 73

M	A	R	E		A	C	H	E		S	O	P
I	R	O	N		L	O	O	N		H	U	E
L	E	N	D		E	M	U	S		E	R	R
L	A	S	S	O		P	R	U	N	E		
			B	R	A		E	A	R	L	S	
A	D	S		O	U	S	T		B	E	E	T
S	I	P		E	S	S	E	S		S	E	A
K	E	E	P		H	I	N	T		T	R	Y
S	T	E	A	L		O	D	E				
	D	R	A	W	N		P	H	O	T	O	
A	D	E		R	E	A	P		A	K	I	N
S	I	R		V	E	T	O		L	A	M	E
H	E	S		A	P	E	D		L	Y	E	S

CROSSWORD 74

H	E	W		F	L	I	T		T	O	P	S
O	R	E		L	U	T	E		O	V	A	L
P	R	E	S	E	N	C	E		G	E	N	E
			E	A	C	H		O	A	R	E	D
C	H	I	C		H	Y	M	N				
L	I	S	T			A	L	I	B	I	S	
A	F	L	O	A	T		D	Y	N	A	M	O
P	I	E	R	C	E				L	I	P	S
			E	A	V	E		A	L	S	O	
D	R	A	T	S		A	M	E	N			
R	A	G	E		B	L	E	N	D	E	R	S
E	V	E	N		R	I	N	D		R	A	T
W	E	D	S		A	D	D	S		A	N	Y

CROSSWORD 75

P	U	M	P		I	N	S		R	A	N	G
A	S	E	A		T	O	E		O	B	O	E
R	E	S	T		S	W	E	E	T	E	S	T
T	R	A	C	K			W	A	D	E	S	
		H	E	A	D	S	E	T				
R	I	D		P	R	E	P		E	T	C	H
A	C	E		T	O	P	A	Z		H	U	E
Y	E	W	S		S	O	D	A		Y	E	S
	P	R	E	T	E	N	D					
I	G	L	O	O			E	A	T	E	N	
D	O	O	R	B	E	L	L		D	O	V	E
L	O	U	T		B	E	E		D	R	E	W
E	N	D	S		B	I	G		Y	E	N	S

CROSSWORD 76

W	H	O	A		S	P	A		R	E	E	F
H	E	M	S		A	R	C		E	A	V	E
O	R	E	S		T	O	E		D	R	E	W
M	E	N	U			S	P	Y				
		M	E	S	S		R	E	S	E	E	
A	T	T	E	N	T	I	V	E		P	A	Y
L	A	Y		A	I	D	E	S		U	S	E
A	L	P		C	R	E	A	T	U	R	E	S
S	C	O	T	T		S	L	O	P			
		A	S	P					R	U	B	S
O	W	E	S		E	R	A		O	R	A	L
W	O	N	T		S	A	G		O	G	L	E
L	O	D	E		T	W	O		T	E	E	D

360

CROSSWORD 77

M	A	N	█	S	H	E	█	M	O	C	H	A
A	G	E	█	H	E	N	█	E	T	H	I	C
R	O	W	B	O	A	T	█	T	H	E	R	E
█	█	U	N	T	I	L	█	E	W	E	S	█
P	E	K	O	E	█	R	E	A	R	█	█	█
A	C	H	Y	█	F	E	A	R	█	A	W	E
C	H	A	S	E	R	█	P	E	S	T	E	R
E	O	N	█	G	I	S	T	█	H	O	E	R
█	█	O	G	L	E	█	R	A	M	P	S	█
M	O	S	T	█	L	I	T	E	R	█	█	█
O	M	I	T	S	█	Z	I	P	P	E	R	S
M	E	L	E	E	█	E	E	L	█	Y	O	U
S	N	O	R	T	█	D	R	Y	█	E	B	B

CROSSWORD 78

A	F	T	█	D	A	F	T	█	█	A	W	L
C	R	Y	█	I	C	I	E	R	█	P	R	O
T	O	P	█	A	R	E	N	A	█	R	I	D
█	█	I	D	L	E	R	█	P	R	O	S	E
D	E	C	O	█	█	C	L	I	E	N	T	S
O	R	A	L	█	H	E	E	D	S	█	█	█
G	A	L	L	E	Y	█	A	S	I	D	E	S
█	█	█	A	D	M	A	N	█	D	E	L	L
S	C	O	R	I	N	G	█	U	G	L	Y	█
T	R	U	S	T	█	E	L	D	E	R	█	█
R	A	T	█	O	W	N	E	R	█	E	W	E
A	T	E	█	R	O	D	E	O	█	E	O	N
P	E	R	█	█	E	A	R	P	█	S	O	D

CROSSWORD 79

S	W	A	P	█	G	E	M	█	C	H	A	R
I	O	T	A	█	E	V	A	█	H	O	L	E
T	E	E	N	█	N	I	T	█	U	P	O	N
█	█	D	W	E	L	T	█	B	E	E	T	█
B	A	Z	A	A	R	█	E	B	B	█	█	█
A	L	E	█	F	A	R	█	L	Y	I	N	G
I	T	S	█	F	L	A	R	E	█	D	O	E
T	O	T	A	L	█	T	E	A	█	L	E	T
█	█	P	E	R	█	A	C	C	E	S	S	█
S	H	O	P	█	I	T	C	H	Y	█	█	█
P	A	P	A	█	V	A	T	█	C	R	A	B
O	V	A	L	█	A	P	E	█	L	A	C	E
T	E	L	L	█	L	E	D	█	E	Y	E	D

CROSSWORD 80

T	U	T	U	█	H	E	M	█	A	L	T	O
O	P	E	N	█	I	V	Y	█	S	E	A	L
T	O	N	S	█	M	E	N	█	K	I	N	D
E	N	S	U	E	█	█	A	L	E	█	█	█
█	█	█	R	A	T	S	█	E	R	E	C	T
M	A	T	E	R	I	A	L	S	█	G	O	O
I	R	E	█	M	E	N	U	S	█	O	R	E
T	E	A	█	A	D	D	R	E	S	S	E	S
T	A	M	E	R	█	S	E	N	T	█	█	█
█	█	S	K	Y	█	█	S	A	T	I	N	█
A	C	E	S	█	A	F	T	█	R	I	D	E
T	O	G	A	█	W	O	O	█	C	R	E	W
E	D	G	Y	█	N	E	T	█	H	E	A	T

CROSSWORD 81

S	H	A	H		C	L	A	D		T	A	B
H	U	L	A		H	O	B	O		A	X	E
Y	E	L	L		A	T	O	M		I	L	L
		F	O	R		V	I	O	L	E	T	
B	U	S		U	R	G	E	N	T			
A	P	P	A	R	E	L		O	H	A	R	A
B	O	I	L		D	A	B		E	P	I	C
E	N	T	E	R		R	E	F	R	E	S	H
		R	E	P	E	A	L		S	K	Y	
P	A	S	T	O	R		R	Y	E			
I	C	E		P	O	P	E		A	B	L	E
E	R	A		E	V	E	R		V	A	I	N
S	E	T		N	E	W	S		E	Y	E	D

CROSSWORD 82

M	O	S	S		S	N	O	W		G	A	P
A	N	T	E		T	I	D	E		A	D	O
S	C	A	N		O	L	D	T	I	M	E	R
H	E	M	S		W	E	B		N	E	S	T
		P	E	P		A	F	T				
A	C	E		R	A	I	L	R	O	A	D	S
D	U	D		U	N	C	L	E		P	I	E
S	P	E	E	D	I	E	S	T		P	E	W
	G	E	M		S	I	R					
S	H	A	G		A	S	H		T	O	S	S
C	A	S	S	E	T	T	E		E	V	E	N
A	L	E		W	E	A	R		M	A	M	A
B	O	A		E	D	G	E		S	L	I	P

CROSSWORD 83

P	A	W	S		A	C	H	E		F	A	D
R	I	O	T		D	U	E	L		L	I	E
O	D	O	R		S	T	A	B		A	L	E
F	E	L	I	X		D	O	O	M			
		C	R	A	M		W	A	I	T	S	
I	M	I	T	A	T	E	D		K	N	E	E
R	E	D		Y	O	D	E	L		G	E	M
O	M	E	N		M	A	C	A	R	O	N	I
N	O	N	O	S		L	O	V	E			
		T	W	I	G		A	N	T	I	C	
L	E	I		G	R	I	T		T	A	C	O
O	A	T		H	A	R	E		A	M	E	N
T	R	Y		T	Y	K	E		L	E	S	S

CROSSWORD 84

S	T	U	D		T	R	I	M		C	O	W
A	W	R	Y		R	U	D	E		A	D	E
S	I	G	N		U	N	E	A	R	N	E	D
S	T	E	A	L	S		A	T	E			
		M	E	T	A	L		A	M	I	D	
B	E	L	O	V	E	D		R	O	S	Y	
A	C	E		Y	E	A	S	T		A	L	E
S	H	A	G		P	L	A	T	T	E	R	
S	O	F	A		S	T	Y	L	E			
		R	A	T		N	E	A	R	B	Y	
L	A	D	Y	L	I	K	E		C	O	R	E
O	R	E		O	N	E	S		U	P	O	N
W	E	B		E	G	G	S		P	E	W	S

CROSSWORD 85

```
S C A T █ A T O M █ R Y E
A R C H █ N I N E █ O A R
G O N E █ T E E N █ S P A
S P E E C H █ S U R E █ █
█ █ █ H I S █ █ E B B S █
D A B █ I L L █ A D U L T
I C E █ C L E A N █ S U E
S H A R K █ E L K █ H E M
H E R O █ █ P A L █ █ █ █
█ █ A D O S █ R E S T E D
C A B █ W H O M █ L A V A
O I L █ L O R E █ O P E N
O D E █ S E E D █ B E R G
```

CROSSWORD 86

```
B I A S █ V E T █ B E G S
A R C H █ A X E █ R E E K
C O R E █ L A M █ A L L Y
K N E E █ I M P L Y █ █ █
█ █ █ N O D █ E S S A Y █
W E T █ Y A R D S █ T W O
I V Y █ S T I E S █ A R K
N I P █ T E P E E █ R Y E
G L O V E █ █ P R O █ █ █
█ █ I R A T E █ W H I P █
N E S S █ U R N █ N I C E
A R E A █ T O E █ E V E R
B R A S █ O D D █ D E S K
```

CROSSWORD 87

```
A W E D █ V A N █ C H A R
C O V E █ I C E █ R O P E
T O I L █ D E T A I L E D
█ █ L I F E █ D E E D S █
C A N █ L O A F E R █ █ █
L I E █ O G L E █ S M U G
A D S █ G A L A S █ A N Y
M E S S █ M O T H █ R I M
█ █ T E E T H E █ I T S █
A D O R E █ E D E N █ █ █
B E W I L D E R █ M A N E
L A N D █ A Y E █ I D O L
E L S E █ B E D █ T E R M
```

CROSSWORD 88

```
A D E S █ B A S S █ T O O
C O L A █ R U I N █ A N D
N E S T █ A T T A I N E D
E R E C T █ H E I R █ █ █
█ █ █ H O B O █ L E A S T
E M P E R O R S █ █ C O O
P O O L E D █ O P E R A S
I T S █ █ Y O D E L E R S
C H E E K █ P A G E █ █ █
█ █ █ S I Z E █ S C R A P
M O I S T E N S █ T A X I
O W N █ T R E E █ O V E N
D E N █ Y O R E █ R E S T
```

CROSSWORD 89

```
T B A R | W O O | S U N G
A R C H Y | R U G | A S E A
R A C Y | E R R | L E T S
S T O M P S | E S S |
| M E L T S | C A C H E
A S P | A L O H A | A I R
S P A | T E N O R | S K I
K I N | T R I A L | S E E
S T Y L E | C R E P E |
| I R K | S T U R D Y
B R A N | E Y E | P O R E
R U L E | G A L | P L E A
A M E N | S K Y | Y E W S
```

CROSSWORD 90

```
M I S T | W A S | S T O W
E C H O | R I P | C A M E
M E A T | I R E | A C E D
O D D E S T | N Y L O N S
| I M I T A T E D |
A D E | P E P | T E R M S
R U S T | N I P | D E A L
M O T I F | N A G | A N Y
| D I A G R A M S |
I N F I R M | C L A S P S
R I L E | A S H | C U R E
O N E S | S E E | A R E A
N E X T | S A D | W E P T
```

CROSSWORD 91

```
B R A | S P A R | R A M S
O A R | E L S E | A L I T
G Y M | L I S P | N O N E
| O G L E | L A G O O N
A W R Y | S W I G | F R O
D E E P | H E E L |
O D D S | S A D | E C H O
| Y O W L | T O U R
H I S | P E E K | U R G E
I N C I T E | I M P S |
P L A N | T A T A | A N D
P A R K | E W E S | G O O
O W E S | N E S T | E G G
```

CROSSWORD 92

```
M A G | S O D A | D O M E
I C Y | I R O N | O V E R
D E M A N D E D | N E A R
| U S E | A N T S
R A F T | R E A C T |
I G L O O | M I L E A G E
P E A | B R I D E | I L L
E D G E O U T | F O R U M
| S E N S E | R Y E S
S W A T | A P E |
A R I A | S T R E S S E S
G E N T | O I L S | A L P
A N T E | B E S T | P L Y
```

CROSSWORD 93

J	E	T		U	P	O	N		L	O	S	T
I	R	E		S	O	M	E		A	B	L	E
B	R	A	C	E	L	E	T		T	O	E	S
		O	R	A	L		S	H	E	E	T	
A	S	P	S		R	E	A	P		S	T	Y
D	I	E	T	S		T	I	E	S			
S	C	R	A	W	L		L	E	T	H	A	L
		R	A	Y	S		D	R	A	P	E	
S	A	W		R	E	E	D		A	G	E	D
A	L	A	R	M		A	R	M	Y			
L	I	K	E		P	L	E	A	S	A	N	T
A	B	E	D		R	E	A	R		C	O	O
D	I	N	O		O	D	D	S		T	R	Y

CROSSWORD 94

S	H	Y		E	L	S	E		M	A	T	S
W	O	E		Y	A	P	S		O	P	A	L
A	L	L		E	R	R	S		D	E	N	Y
T	Y	P	O		G	E	E	S	E			
			C	R	E	A	S	E		L	A	D
D	I	S	C	A	R	D		A	G	O	N	Y
I	N	P	U	T			S	A	U	T	E	
S	T	A	R	T		S	M	O	L	D	E	R
H	L	N		A	T	T	U	N	E			
		S	N	O	R	T		S	E	A	M	
S	A	F	E		K	I	T	E		D	U	O
K	N	E	E		E	V	E	N		I	T	S
I	T	E	M		N	E	R	D		T	O	T

CROSSWORD 95

E	V	E	S		M	A	S		I	R	I	S
O	I	N	K		A	L	P		N	I	C	E
N	A	T	I	O	N	A	L		S	L	E	W
S	L	I	E	R		S	I	T	T	E	R	S
		T	R	A	Y		T	I	E			
G	A	L		L	E	T		S	A	F	E	S
E	W	E	S		N	U	T		D	I	R	E
M	E	D	I	C		G	A	P		R	A	T
		L	O	T		D	U	P	E			
S	T	E	E	P	E	R		R	E	S	O	W
H	Y	M	N		M	E	A	L	T	I	M	E
E	P	I	C		P	A	N		A	D	E	S
D	O	T	E		T	R	Y		L	E	N	T

CROSSWORD 96

B	A	T		A	W	L		D	E	C	A	Y
A	R	E		S	H	E		A	D	O	R	E
R	E	A	C	H	E	D		T	I	N	T	S
B	A	S	H		E	G	R	E	T	S		
		A	L	L	E	Y		U	S	E		
S	H	A	M	E		R	E	D		M	O	B
P	E	N	P	A	L		S	U	P	E	R	B
A	R	C		P	E	P		C	A	R	T	S
T	O	E		N	E	C	K	S				
		S	A	D	D	E	R		S	O	S	O
R	E	T	I	E		R	I	P	E	N	E	D
E	R	O	D	E		E	E	L		C	E	E
F	A	R	E	D		D	R	Y		E	S	S

CROSSWORD 97

C	A	F	E	■	S	K	I	■	S	C	A	M
O	I	L	Y	■	K	I	T	■	T	U	N	E
B	L	U	E	■	I	N	S	■	A	R	T	S
■	■	S	O	N	G	■	E	L	V	E	S	■
C	O	C	O	A	■	K	A	L	E	■	■	■
A	P	A	R	T	M	E	N	T	■	B	A	R
M	E	R	E	■	A	L	E	■	T	A	C	O
E	N	D	■	B	A	K	E	S	A	L	E	S
■	■	B	R	I	M	■	■	P	U	L	S	E
A	B	O	U	T	■	S	W	A	N	■	■	■
L	E	A	N	■	S	H	E	■	T	A	B	S
T	A	R	T	■	P	O	P	■	E	X	I	T
O	D	D	S	■	Y	E	T	■	D	E	N	Y

CROSSWORD 98

L	E	A	F	■	S	P	A	■	P	L	O	T
E	A	V	E	■	U	R	N	■	H	A	R	E
T	R	A	N	S	M	I	T	■	O	X	E	N
S	L	I	C	E	■	M	E	A	T	■	■	■
■	■	L	E	E	R	■	■	S	O	L	E	D
B	R	A	■	E	D	G	E	■	I	V	Y	■
R	I	B	■	V	I	O	L	A	■	F	E	E
E	L	L	■	I	N	T	O	■	E	R	R	■
W	E	E	P	S	■	■	B	U	T	S	■	■
■	■	R	A	S	P	■	■	S	H	A	R	D
M	I	D	I	■	M	A	N	E	U	V	E	R
A	C	I	D	■	O	N	E	■	M	E	N	U
T	Y	P	E	■	G	E	T	■	P	R	O	M

CROSSWORD 99

I	M	P	S	■	D	O	N	S	■	N	E	W
R	I	L	E	■	W	O	O	L	■	A	X	E
K	N	O	W	L	E	D	G	E	■	P	E	R
S	I	T	■	E	L	L	■	P	A	S	S	E
■	■	■	A	L	E	R	T	S	■	■	■	■
A	P	T	■	V	I	S	E	■	P	A	I	R
N	E	A	T	E	N	■	M	U	S	C	L	E
T	A	X	I	■	G	R	I	T	■	E	L	F
■	■	■	R	E	S	E	N	T	■	■	■	■
C	R	U	E	L	■	A	D	E	■	T	A	R
R	A	P	■	U	N	D	E	R	T	A	K	E
A	G	O	■	D	O	E	R	■	A	C	I	D
M	E	N	■	E	R	R	S	■	B	O	N	D

CROSSWORD 100

D	R	A	T	■	T	A	P	■	C	L	A	P
I	O	T	A	■	O	I	L	■	H	O	P	E
S	L	O	T	■	A	D	E	■	I	C	E	R
K	E	P	T	■	S	E	A	■	L	A	S	T
■	■	■	O	P	T	■	S	K	I	T	■	■
B	A	Y	O	U	■	H	E	N	■	I	T	S
E	W	E	■	S	W	E	D	E	■	N	A	P
T	E	A	■	H	I	M	■	A	N	G	R	Y
■	■	R	A	Y	S	■	O	D	E	■	■	■
B	A	N	S	■	H	E	W	■	T	R	A	M
I	R	I	S	■	F	A	N	■	T	A	C	O
D	I	N	E	■	U	S	E	■	E	C	H	O
S	A	G	S	■	L	E	D	■	D	E	E	R

CROSSWORD 101

H	A	D		S	T	E	M		P	L	A	N
E	Y	E		C	O	L	A		R	A	C	E
S	E	A		A	R	M	Y		E	R	R	S
	D	A	M	P		B	A	S	K	E	T	
G	O	L	D		E	V	E	N	T			
E	P	I	S	O	D	E		T	O	O	T	H
M	A	N		F	O	R	D	S		V	E	E
S	L	E	E	T		S	O	Y	B	E	A	N
		R	E	P	E	L		I	R	K	S	
B	A	N	A	N	A		L	I	T	E		
O	R	E	S		S	P	A	N		A	D	D
D	I	C	E		T	A	R	T		S	U	E
Y	A	K	S		A	L	S	O		Y	E	W

CROSSWORD 102

P	U	S	S		L	E	S	S		R	A	T
A	N	T	E		O	R	A	L		E	Y	E
T	I	R	E		T	R	I	O		F	E	E
S	T	U	M	P		A	D	O	B	E		
Y	E	T		U	R	N		P	U	R	E	E
				R	U	D	E		M	E	R	E
S	T	E	E	R	S		A	P	P	E	A	L
H	A	L	T		H	A	R	E				
E	R	E	C	T		E	L	L		C	A	P
		C	H	E	E	R		T	H	O	S	E
P	O	T		A	C	I	D		O	N	C	E
E	W	E		C	H	A	R		O	D	O	R
A	N	D		H	O	L	Y		D	O	T	S

CROSSWORD 103

C	A	R	S		A	C	T		B	L	U	R
O	R	A	L		T	O	O		E	A	S	E
A	C	C	I	D	E	N	T		A	P	E	D
T	H	E	M	E		S	E	A	R			
		H	E	A	R	T		D	E	B	T	S
L	E	O		F	E	E		D	R	O	O	P
Y	A	R	D		F	L	Y		S	A	G	E
E	S	S	E	S		L	E	D		R	A	W
S	T	E	N	O		A	W	A	R	D		
			S	P	O	T		R	E	G	A	L
R	A	T	E		N	I	C	K	N	A	M	E
I	C	E	S		C	O	O		E	M	I	T
M	E	E	T		E	N	D		W	E	D	S

CROSSWORD 104

S	M	O	G		F	O	A	L		A	T	E
H	I	V	E		I	D	L	E		F	I	N
O	M	E	N		D	E	T	E	S	T	E	D
P	E	R	I	O	D		A	R	E			
			A	W	L		R	E	A	L	M	S
S	T	A	L	L	E	D		D	R	O	O	P
A	R	M		R	Y	E			F	L	U	
S	E	I	N	E		E	X	I	S	T	E	D
S	E	D	A	N	S		P	R	O			
			V	A	T		R	E	C	U	R	S
P	L	A	Y	M	A	T	E		K	N	E	E
E	A	R		E	R	A	S		E	D	I	T
A	P	T		L	E	N	S		T	O	N	S

CROSSWORD 105

E	C	H	O		A	S	H		A	L	T	O
R	E	A	P		C	U	E		S	A	I	L
A	N	T	E	A	T	E	R		S	P	E	D
S	T	E	R	N			T	O	T	E		
			A	D	S			O	T	H	E	R
A	L	A	S		H	A	Y	S		A	X	E
C	O	N		H	A	L	O	S		L	A	B
I	C	E		U	G	L	Y		G	E	M	S
D	O	W	E	L			O	A	R			
			B	A	S	S		L	O	O	S	E
B	L	O	B		T	A	K	E	O	V	E	R
R	O	D	E		A	G	E		V	E	E	R
A	P	E	D		B	A	Y		E	N	D	S

CROSSWORD 106

B	R	O	S		O	R	A	L		A	N	D
L	U	G	E		P	O	R	E		J	O	Y
A	B	L	E		T	W	I	T		A	P	E
H	Y	E	N	A			S	T	A	R	E	D
				R	E	D	E	E	M			
S	L	O	T	C	A	R		R	U	M	B	A
P	A	R	E		R	A	Y		S	E	A	T
A	M	E	N	S		P	A	L	E	T	T	E
			S	C	H	E	M	E				
S	E	V	E	R	E		D	R	I	F	T	
O	W	E		E	A	S	E		O	N	L	Y
F	E	E		E	V	E	R		A	T	O	P
A	S	P		N	E	A	R		M	O	P	E

CROSSWORD 107

A	N	D		A	C	E	S		P	R	O	D
P	E	R		J	O	L	T		A	I	D	E
T	W	O		A	B	L	E		S	T	O	W
		P	U	R	R		E	A	T	E	R	Y
A	I	L	S		A	S	P	S				
C	R	E	E	P		W	E	T		E	L	K
H	I	T		A	F	I	R	E		V	E	E
E	S	S		Y	E	S		R	E	I	G	N
			E	A	S	T		A	L	S	O	
R	E	P	O	R	T		E	A	R	N		
A	V	I	D		H	A	N	G		E	L	M
T	E	E	D		E	L	S	E		S	E	E
E	R	R	S		R	E	E	D		S	I	T

CROSSWORD 108

S	W	I	G		M	O	M		A	R	I	D
P	O	L	E		A	P	E		B	O	R	E
Y	E	L	L		Y	E	A		U	P	O	N
			A	L	O	N	G		T	E	N	T
P	A	S	T	E		E	E	L	S			
U	N	L	I	T		D	R	Y		R	U	B
S	T	I	N	T			R	A	I	S	E	
H	E	M		E	S	S		I	D	L	E	D
			G	R	I	T		C	H	E	S	S
C	H	A	R		E	R	A	S	E			
H	A	L	E		S	A	W		R	E	B	S
E	L	S	E		T	I	E		E	V	I	L
F	O	O	T		A	N	D		D	E	N	Y

368

CROSSWORD 109

```
C O B . S O A R . D I S C
A P E   I D L E .   A S E A
R E F   P E E P .   T O W N
P R O P S   R E G A L .
S A G A .   T A N .   A W L
.   P R E S T O .   T E E
S T R A I N .   E M C E E D
H O E   S T E R E O .
E O N   E R A .   L A V A
.   T U N A S .   V A P O R
I R I S .   N I C E .   A G E
C A N E .   C L U E .   R U N
E G G S .   E Y E S .   T E A
```

CROSSWORD 110

```
A J A R .   L O P .   B L O B
D A T A .   E A R .   L O G O
D Y E D .   F R O .   E A R N
.     A N T .   P I N N E D
S W O R E .   F O N D .
O A K .   C R O S S .   E B B
B R A .   K A R A T .   C O O
S T Y .   T I T L E .   H A D
.     L I N E .   A R O S E
I S S U E D .   O D E .
O P E N .   R A N .   F I F E
W I N G .   O I L .   E V E S
A N T E .   P R Y .   R Y E S
```

CROSSWORD 111

```
S T I R .   C U D .   V I L E
C U T E .   O N E .   I R I S
A B E D .   P I E .   N E T S
N A M E .   T R O Y .
.     E L F .   P L A N T
M A R M A L A D E .   N O R
A C E .   B A R O N .   T O O
A R E .   E X C E L L E N T
M E D A L .   R Y E .
.     U S E D .   E D I T
A V I D .   A I D .   R I C E
S E M I .   S K I .   E V E N
K E P T .   Y E N .   D A D S
```

CROSSWORD 112

```
G A Y .   D R A W .   A S P S
E W E .   Y U L E .   W H E T
L E S S E N E D .   H U L A
.     U R N .   G R I T T Y
S A G E .   I D E A L .
O I L .   O N E .   T E N T H
F R O .   A G E N T .   O R E
T Y P O S .   M A Y .   S E A
.     B E A S T .   P E E R
O B S E S S .   I C E .
G R A Y .   S A V A G E L Y
L A M E .   E X E S .   B E E
E Y E D .   T E S T .   B I T
```

369

CROSSWORD 113

H	A	R	M	■	I	V	E	S	■	W	H	O
A	R	E	A	■	M	I	R	E	■	E	O	N
S	C	A	M	■	M	E	R	E	■	E	L	L
■	■	W	A	D	E	■	D	A	D	D	Y	■
S	P	A	■	O	D	D	E	S	T	■	■	■
W	O	K	■	R	I	O	T	■	E	E	L	S
A	R	E	■	M	A	N	E	D	■	N	I	L
M	E	N	U	■	T	O	R	E	■	D	O	E
■	■	S	T	E	R	N	S	■	A	N	D	■
S	P	R	E	E	■	■	A	K	I	N	■	■
T	I	E	■	P	O	L	L	■	O	G	R	E
U	P	S	■	I	D	O	L	■	T	E	A	S
N	E	T	■	D	E	W	Y	■	A	R	T	S

CROSSWORD 114

S	H	E	■	S	E	A	S	■	L	A	S	T
W	O	N	■	T	A	X	I	■	A	N	E	W
A	R	C	■	O	R	E	S	■	M	I	N	I
P	R	O	M	P	T	■	■	M	A	N	■	■
S	I	R	E	■	H	O	O	F	■	A	T	E
■	D	E	L	I	■	M	A	R	B	L	E	■
■	E	M	P	E	R	O	R	■	■	■	■	■
■	D	E	E	P	E	N	■	M	I	S	S	■
F	O	X	■	S	A	S	S	■	E	A	C	H
A	L	P	■	■	■	T	O	F	F	E	E	■
S	L	I	D	■	S	H	O	W	■	A	N	D
T	O	R	E	■	P	I	N	E	■	R	I	G
S	P	E	W	■	A	P	E	D	■	I	C	E

CROSSWORD 115

A	W	E	S	■	F	L	I	P	■	D	A	M
S	O	R	T	■	L	I	C	E	■	A	T	E
H	E	R	O	■	O	P	E	R	A	T	O	R
■	N	A	G	■	■	■	C	A	M	E	■	■
S	H	E	E	N	■	G	L	E	E	■	■	■
L	O	W	■	G	R	O	U	N	D	H	O	G
A	P	E	■	L	A	R	G	E	■	A	D	E
M	E	S	S	E	N	G	E	R	■	L	E	T
■	■	U	R	G	E	■	G	R	O	S	S	■
B	O	R	E	■	■	D	Y	E	■	■	■	■
I	N	I	T	I	A	T	E	■	A	F	A	R
A	C	T	■	L	Y	E	S	■	L	O	G	O
S	E	E	■	L	E	E	K	■	M	E	E	T

CROSSWORD 116

M	A	P	■	S	P	E	D	■	L	I	M	B
O	I	L	■	T	O	N	E	■	O	R	A	L
A	D	E	■	R	E	D	S	■	N	O	T	E
T	E	A	P	O	T	■	S	I	G	N	E	D
■	■	A	N	S	W	E	R	■	■	■	■	■
A	P	I	N	G	■	E	R	E	C	T	E	D
N	I	L	E	■	K	I	T	■	H	A	L	O
Y	E	L	L	I	N	G	■	S	A	B	L	E
■	■	M	O	H	A	I	R	■	■	■	■	■
A	B	R	U	P	T	■	R	E	T	O	L	D
C	O	O	S	■	T	W	I	G	■	W	O	E
I	D	L	E	■	E	A	S	E	■	N	O	W
D	E	E	D	■	D	Y	E	S	■	S	K	Y

CROSSWORD 117

S	H	I	N		B	I	B	S		A	D	S
L	O	N	E		O	M	I	T		W	O	O
A	U	T	O		S	P	R	A	W	L	E	D
W	R	O	N	G	S		D	Y	E			
		R	I	B			L	O	A	D
E	L	K		E	E	L		S	L	O	P	E
T	O	N		E	R	U	P	T		Z	E	E
C	R	E	A	K		S	U	E		E	S	S
H	E	E	D		H	E	N			
	D	A	Y		B	O	O	M	E	D
N	E	W	S	R	E	E	L		W	E	A	R
A	W	E		M	A	Y	O		L	A	V	A
B	E	D		S	H	E	S		S	T	E	M

CROSSWORD 118

E	A	V	E		A	C	T	S		A	D	E
L	I	E	N		S	L	A	W		B	R	A
F	L	E	A		P	A	P	A		L	E	T
	M	O	S	S		B	R	E	W	S
T	R	E	E	D		S	O	S	O	
B	U	L	L	E	T	I	N		T	A	N	G
A	L	S		S	A	F	E	S		C	O	O
R	E	E	D		L	I	S	T	E	N	E	D
	O	G	L	E		A	X	E	L	S
T	I	L	E	R		D	A	R	T	
W	O	O		O	P	A	L		E	B	B	S
I	T	S		W	I	D	E		N	O	O	K
G	A	S		L	E	S	S		T	A	X	I

CROSSWORD 119

S	A	G	A		O	F	F		C	O	A	L
E	L	L	S		A	I	R		A	I	D	E
A	T	O	P		T	E	E		B	L	E	D
R	O	B	E			R	E	E	L	
	C	R	O	C		N	E	A	R	S
S	T	A	T	E	M	E	N	T		L	O	P
H	A	S	S	L	E		A	R	C	A	D	E
A	L	E		I	N	C	R	E	A	S	E	D
G	L	A	S	S		A	Y	E	S	
	K	H	A	N		T	H	E	N
G	A	L	A		L	O	W		L	I	M	E
U	N	I	T		S	E	E		E	D	I	T
T	Y	P	E		O	D	D		S	E	T	S

CROSSWORD 120

L	A	I	R		S	E	L	F		N	A	P
A	C	R	E		T	E	A	L		E	W	E
M	E	E	T		A	L	S	O		G	E	T
	I	N	N		H	O	B	O		
	S	P	E	E	D	S		R	E	T	A	R
F	O	R		S	A	K	E		A	I	D	E
E	L	E	C	T	R	I	C	T	R	A	I	N
L	A	V	A		D	E	L	I		T	O	T
T	R	E	N	D		S	I	E	G	E	S	
	N	E	E	D		P	R	O		
A	C	T		P	A	Y	S		O	B	O	E
D	O	E		T	R	E	E		E	R	A	S
S	O	D		H	E	N	S		Y	A	K	S

CROSSWORD 121

H	U	M	P		S	T	U	B		F	I	B
O	R	A	L		W	I	P	E		A	R	E
O	G	R	E		U	N	S	A	L	T	E	D
D	E	T	A	I	N		C	U	E			
			D	O	G	M	A		T	E	R	M
T	W	I	S	T		O	L	D		P	I	E
E	O	N		A	P	T	E	R		I	C	E
A	R	T		S	A	T		Y	A	C	H	T
S	M	O	G		R	O	B	E	D			
			A	F	T		E	R	O	D	E	S
P	E	R	S	O	N	A	L		R	E	A	P
A	W	E		R	E	D	O		E	L	S	E
W	E	D		D	R	E	W		S	L	E	W

CROSSWORD 122

T	O	M		T	E	A	M		F	I	T	S
E	W	E		A	X	L	E		E	C	H	O
A	N	D		K	I	L	N		L	E	A	N
			I	R	I	S		T	W	I	S	T	S
A	C	C	E	N	T		H	E	X			
C	L	I	N	G		W	O	E		C	O	B
R	A	N	T		E	E	L		M	A	N	E
E	Y	E		A	C	T		D	A	N	C	E
			P	R	O		L	I	S	T	E	N
U	N	S	E	E	N		L	A	K	E		
S	A	P	S		O	V	A	L		E	S	S
E	M	I	T		M	I	M	E		N	U	T
D	E	N	S		Y	E	A	R		S	P	Y

CROSSWORD 123

L	A	R	K		L	A	V	A		S	O	P
I	R	O	N		A	M	E	N		H	U	E
T	R	U	E		D	I	E	T		E	R	R
E	A	T	E	N		D	R	I	L	L		
R	Y	E		E	S	S		S	A	L	S	A
			O	A	T	H		M	A	I	D	
A	P	R	O	N	S		E	J	E	C	T	S
P	R	I	M		H	E	R	O				
T	O	N	E	D		A	S	H		A	R	T
		S	N	E	E	R		N	E	W	E	R
L	E	I		C	A	N	T		M	A	T	E
U	R	N		A	S	E	A		I	R	I	S
G	A	G		F	E	R	N		T	E	E	S

CROSSWORD 124

P	L	E	A		A	D	S		A	M	M	O
R	I	D	S		C	O	O		R	E	A	D
I	M	I	T	A	T	E	D		C	A	K	E
M	O	T	E	L		R	A	T	E	S		
			R	E	C	E	D	E	D			
T	W	I	N		H	A	R	V	E	S	T	S
W	E	T		D	O	T	E	S		O	A	K
O	B	S	C	U	R	E	S		S	P	R	Y
			U	T	E	N	S	I	L			
D	O	W	R	Y			N	O	S	E	D	
A	B	E	L		B	E	A	N	P	O	L	E
S	O	R	E		U	R	N		E	A	S	E
H	E	E	D		T	R	Y		S	P	E	D

CROSSWORD 125

```
B A S E   A R T S   S O Y
A T O M   R E E K   I R E
R O D E   E C L I P S E S
S P A N K   A L S O
      D E L L   L A T H
A P T   P U L P   A C H E
S I E S T A   E E R I E R
P L A N   U S E D   D E B
S E M I   A K I N
      F E L L   T A L K S
U N A F R A I D   V I N E
P E N   A N N E   E M I T
S T Y   S E E N   L O T S
```

CROSSWORD 126

```
S A P   S C A N   P R O M
L I E   A U T O   E A V E
A D E   L E E R   A G E S
W E L D S   A R E N A
      R A S C A L
F R A Y   L O L L I P O P
R I P E   A C E   V E I L
O P E R A T O R   O N L Y
      N E A T E R
A S S E T   N Y L O N
W H O A   O W E D   O R E
R E A R   F O R E   C A R
Y A K S   F E A R   O L D
```

CROSSWORD 127

```
S P A R   S O A R   S A D
T A L E   T I L E   P R Y
I R A Q   U L T I M A T E
R E S U L T   O N E
      I O T A S   T U S K
S H O R T E R   P A N
T I R E   R E F   D O V E
E R A   N O M I N E E
M E L T   G A L A S
      O A R   D R A M A S
P L A Y M A T E   R A C K
E E L   I C E R   M I N I
A T E   D E N S   S L E D
```

CROSSWORD 128

```
S L A W   E B B S   A S P
P I L E   N O U N   B A A
Y E A R   T O G O   O W N
      R E L I T   B O D E S
E L M   I C E   V E R Y
A Y E   F I E S T A
R E D D E N   W E L D E D
      A R G U E S   E R A
B R A T   P A T   F R Y
R E C A P   S T Y L E
A R T   A C H E   O N E S
C U E   P O O R   A S E A
E N D   A N T S   F E L T
```

CROSSWORD 129

A	W	A	Y		S	H	I	P		A	L	L
D	A	L	E		T	A	M	E		T	E	E
D	R	E	W		A	B	A	N	D	O	N	S
			S	P	R	I	G		O	P	T	S
L	I	P		R	E	T	E	L	L			
O	R	A	T	O	R		S	A	L	O	O	N
B	I	S	O	N				R	A	D	I	O
E	S	T	A	T	E		S	I	R	E	N	S
		S	O	N	A	T	A		S	K	Y	
S	W	A	T		D	I	R	T	Y			
M	O	I	S	T	U	R	E		E	V	I	L
U	R	N		O	R	E	S		L	I	N	E
G	E	T		W	E	D	S		P	E	N	D

CROSSWORD 130

S	W	A	M		Z	E	E		W	H	A	T
M	E	N	U		A	L	E		A	U	T	O
O	A	T	S		P	E	R		I	T	E	M
G	R	E	E	D		V	I	A	L			
				W	H	E	E	L		S	P	A
B	A	S	T	I	O	N		M	O	O	E	D
A	C	T	I	N	G		H	A	U	L	E	D
T	R	E	E	D		H	U	N	T	E	R	S
H	E	M		L	L	A	M	A				
			T	E	E	N		C	H	I	L	I
D	E	L	I		A	D	S		A	D	A	M
O	R	A	L		F	L	U		S	L	I	P
C	A	G	E		Y	E	N		H	E	R	S

CROSSWORD 131

A	R	C		S	T	U	N		L	E	T	S
T	O	O		P	O	R	E		A	S	I	A
O	B	E	D	I	E	N	T		S	T	E	W
M	E	D	I	C			F	E	E			
			T	E	L	L		A	R	E	N	A
S	P	I	T		O	U	S	T		M	O	B
T	A	C	O		B	R	A		H	E	E	L
A	P	E		K	E	E	L		I	D	L	E
R	A	B	B	I		S	E	C	T			
		E	A	T				A	C	I	D	S
S	I	R	S		S	E	A	S	H	O	R	E
U	R	G	E		P	A	N	T		T	O	N
M	E	S	S		A	R	T	S		A	P	T

CROSSWORD 132

A	N	D		P	R	E	Y		I	M	P	S
C	O	O		E	A	V	E		L	O	R	E
T	R	E	A	T	I	E	S		L	O	O	T
			R	I	D	S		S	E	N	D	S
A	S	S	E	T			P	U	G			
L	O	T		E	S	T	I	M	A	T	E	D
A	R	E	A		W	O	K		L	O	V	E
N	E	W	S	P	A	P	E	R		T	E	A
			T	R	Y			A	M	E	N	D
S	T	O	R	Y		H	U	G	E			
T	A	X	I		N	O	S	I	N	E	S	S
A	C	E	D		A	M	E	N		B	E	T
G	O	N	E		B	E	R	G		B	A	Y

CROSSWORD 133

```
SEEM ADDS  APT
HAVE LYRE  BOA
EVES REEL  LOP
SENATE ALTERS
   WARMER
EPISODE RAJAH
BILL YAP POPE
BELOW ROASTER
   TRAMPS
VESSEL CHOSEN
IRE ALSO DEMO
LAW TEAR OMIT
ESS HYMN RITE
```

CROSSWORD 134

```
HAIR FLU MAMA
ACNE LOT ALAS
TENT AGE SLIP
 UNION OILS
TERROR SONG
OVENS FIX ART
DIM ICILY TOO
OLE LOG GLOBE
 MAYO NEARED
TUBS LYING
ORES EON EDIT
OGRE SUN RULE
TEST TRY SOLE
```

CROSSWORD 135

```
RACY MEMO ARK
OGRE AXED SEE
AREA MIND HAY
SEA FAT POPE
TEMPO SCORED
 DYER PORTER
 REVENUE
 SPIGOT INDY
HOLLOW STEAL
ACES AWE SPA
TIN MAXI NIPS
EAT AILS ORES
SLY PREP REDO
```

CROSSWORD 136

```
SPA STAB CHUM
AIR LODE EASE
DECREASE DYER
 ODD PASSE
DROP SHYER
RIPE TEAR SAW
ICED OAR BLUR
PEN WORD LATE
 VOLTS UPON
SIMON TIE
EDIT STIRRERS
TONE PECK YOU
SLID YAKS EBB
```

CROSSWORD 137

I	T	S		S	H	O	P		A	R	C	S
M	E	T		H	U	L	A		L	O	O	P
P	A	R		R	E	D	S		A	B	L	E
			E	V	E	S		T	H	R	E	A	D
S	T	A	I	D		C	R	A	M			
H	O	M	E	S	T	E	A	D		G	A	L
O	W	E	D		E	L	M		C	L	U	E
E	N	D		R	E	L	I	S	H	I	N	G
			A	U	T	O		L	I	S	T	S
A	L	P	I	N	E		S	E	N	T		
S	A	I	D		R	A	K	E		E	L	F
I	D	L	E		E	X	I	T		N	O	R
A	Y	E	S		D	E	N	Y		S	T	Y

CROSSWORD 138

S	L	A	M		T	A	L	C		L	O	W
T	A	X	I		O	P	A	L		E	R	A
I	C	E	D		R	E	P	O	R	T	E	D
R	E	S	I	G	N		S	P	A			
				R	A	T	E		S	T	E	W
A	F	T		A	D	E		E	P	O	C	H
R	A	W		S	O	N	A	R		S	H	E
T	R	I	O	S		T	W	O		S	O	N
S	E	N	D		S	H	A	D				
			E	A	T		K	E	E	P	E	R
G	E	M	S	T	O	N	E		D	I	V	A
A	Y	E		O	V	E	N		I	T	E	M
P	E	N		P	E	W	S		T	A	R	P

CROSSWORD 139

B	L	A	B		E	B	B		U	R	G	E
Y	O	R	E		B	E	E		N	E	A	R
E	T	C	H		O	A	T		T	E	L	E
			O	W	N		B	O	D	E	S	
V	O	L	L	E	Y	B	A	L	L			
E	X	U	D	E		I	C	E	D	T	E	A
T	E	N		P	A	N	T	S		R	A	W
O	N	G	O	I	N	G		S	T	O	V	E
			I	N	T	E	R	E	S	T	E	D
S	T	U	N	G		A	S	H				
L	A	N	K		P	E	R		I	N	T	O
A	I	D	E		O	R	E		R	A	I	D
P	L	O	D		P	A	R		T	Y	P	E

CROSSWORD 140

S	P	A		H	O	S	S		P	O	D	S
T	I	N		O	B	O	E		E	V	I	L
Y	E	S		W	E	B	S		T	A	K	E
			W	I	L	Y		S	C	A	L	E	D
S	T	E	M		D	I	A	L				
C	A	R	P	S		W	O	N		S	E	A
A	C	E		U	P	E	N	D		T	A	N
R	O	D		G	E	L		Y	E	A	S	T
			E	A	R	L			A	R	T	S
A	L	T	A	R	S		D	A	R	T		
W	O	O	S		I	C	E	D		E	Y	E
L	O	N	E		S	O	M	E		R	O	B
S	P	E	D		T	W	O	S		S	U	B

376

CROSSWORD 141

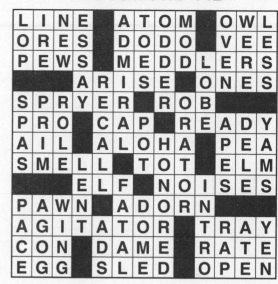

```
T A C T   S T A G   S P Y
A W R Y   P O L O   O L E
B L I P   I N T O   S O N
      T E E N   A S C O T S
A R E   E N T R E E
C A R O L E R     L A S H
E V I L   R A W   L U T E
D E A D   M E L O D I C
      E L A P S E   I R K
C H E R U B   T I R E
H A Y   R O S E   O N E S
O R E   E V E R   A C R E
W E D   D E A N   M E R E
```

CROSSWORD 142

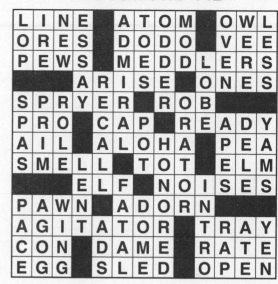

```
L I N E   A T O M   O W L
O R E S   D O D O   V E E
P E W S   M E D D L E R S
      A R I S E   O N E S
S P R Y E R   R O B
P R O   C A P   R E A D Y
A I L   A L O H A   P E A
S M E L L   T O T   E L M
      E L F   N O I S E S
P A W N   A D O R N
A G I T A T O R   T R A Y
C O N   D A M E   R A T E
E G G   S L E D   O P E N
```

CROSSWORD 143

```
R I B   A D E S   F E A T
A G E   F R E T   A L T O
F L A T T I R E   C L E O
T O U R   F I R S T
S O S O   T E N T   N O W
      W A S   S A L I N E
S T R E W     G A P E D
K O A L A S   P E P
Y E T   I N T O   E R R S
      S T A R T   L E A P
C H A T   R O A D S I D E
R O L E   L U T E   G I N
Y E L P   S T O W   N O T
```

CROSSWORD 144

```
A T O M   T A L L   C O W
D O V E   A S E A   A P E
D U E L   S H A W   L A B
S T R E E T   S M E L L S
      D E L I   H A Y
W O O   M E T   N E W E R
A I N T   R A M   S H O O
G L E A M   D I M   A N T
      P U B   S E C T
C I N E M A   U N L E S S
O D E   B R O S   O V A L
D O C   L O D E   M E M O
E L K   E N D S   P R E P
```

CROSSWORD 145

M	E	M	O		I	M	P		O	W	N	S
O	V	A	L		C	O	O		W	H	O	A
W	I	N	D	M	I	L	L		L	I	N	K
S	L	Y		E	N	T	E	R		T	E	E
			B	O	G		C	O	S	T		
E	L	B	O	W		T	A	T	T	L	E	S
L	E	A	N		G	O	T		R	E	N	T
F	I	R	E	A	R	M		B	U	D	D	Y
			I	D	L	E		D	A	M		
A	C	T		L	A	R	R	Y		Z	I	P
W	O	O	F		S	E	A	S	H	O	R	E
L	A	N	E		E	L	K		U	N	I	T
S	L	E	D		D	Y	E		M	E	S	S

CROSSWORD 146

I	M	P		E	P	I	C		B	A	T	H
T	E	A		L	O	C	O		A	C	H	E
S	T	R	O	L	L	E	R		F	R	E	E
		U	S	E		D	E	F	E	N	D	
B	A	R	S		S	I	L	L				
R	I	O	T	S		T	A	V	E	R	N	S
A	R	M		C	H	I	L	I		O	U	T
T	Y	P	H	O	O	N		S	A	B	L	E
		A	U	N	T		Y	E	L	P		
E	N	S	U	R	E		B	Y	E			
R	A	I	L		S	T	R	E	S	S	E	S
R	I	T	E		T	O	O	L		A	R	T
S	L	E	D		Y	O	W	L		W	A	Y

CROSSWORD 147

E	S	S		C	U	B	E		N	A	I	L
G	A	L		O	P	E	N		A	C	N	E
G	L	I	M	P	S	E	S		T	E	N	D
S	E	M	I			T	U	T	U			
			T	W	O		E	R	R	O	R	S
B	L	A	T	A	N	T		E	E	R	I	E
A	I	L		R	E	A	L	M		A	D	E
T	O	T	E	M		N	O	O	D	L	E	S
S	N	O	R	T	S		T	R	Y			
			A	H	E	M		E	Y	E	S	
O	A	T	S		C	O	N	T	R	A	C	T
F	L	E	E		T	R	E	E		W	H	O
F	E	E	D		S	E	W	N		N	O	W

CROSSWORD 148

A	C	H	E		T	W	O		C	H	O	W
C	O	A	X		Y	O	U		R	A	G	E
T	O	D	O		P	O	T		E	L	L	S
			T	O	O	L	S		P	O	E	T
B	A	S	I	N	S		I	C	E			
E	R	E	C	T		O	D	E		H	I	D
S	E	A		I	D	L	E	D		A	D	E
T	A	N		M	O	D		A	P	R	O	N
			P	E	N		F	R	E	E	L	Y
M	E	M	O		A	R	I	S	E			
A	C	E	S		T	O	E		L	I	F	E
S	H	E	S		E	A	R		E	V	E	S
T	O	T	E		D	R	Y		R	Y	E	S

CROSSWORD 149

```
GAZE   FLU   GLOP
OXEN   EAT   HAVE
BEER   ACE   OVER
     OFTEN  SANK
CHILI    SIT
LADLE   VIM   SAW
ELL  SCALP   ODE
FEE   TEN   ACHED
     TAN   CROSS
SASH   STATE
LIKE   OAR   AWAY
IRIS   RUM   TONE
TYPE   STY   ENDS
```

CROSSWORD 150

```
SKIP   SASH   BAR
CONE   AXLE   ORE
RASP   LEER   TIP
ALE   FUSE   EASE
PARROT  KERNEL
  STARES   NAYS
     DESISTS
  SWIG   SHIELD
SCHOOL  ERRORS
TOES   ACRE   CAW
APE   SNUB   SAGA
GEL   OGRE   PLOY
ESS   NEST   YENS
```

CROSSWORD 151

```
CLUB   AGES   RAG
LANE   SOLO   ELL
AIDE   COMB   ATE
PRONTO    BARON
     ETCHER
RIPEN  RADIATE
OVER   CUD   SNOW
DYNAMOS   REDYE
     SOOTHE
STEER    ADORED
LAY   AJAR   DODO
AXE   LODE   EPIC
MID   STEM   SETS
```

CROSSWORD 152

```
FED   BEE   OGLED
AWE   RAN   WHOLE
TENSEST   NOISE
    TWEET   USED
MENU   DRILL
AMONG   TEA   ORE
SIS   APART   VAN
STY   LEI   EMEND
   YAWNS   IRKS
SHOO   SMALL
PANDA   EVADERS
ARCED   NOD   EYE
REELS   TRY   LET
```

CROSSWORD 153

A	M	I	D	■	A	T	O	P	■	B	I	N
B	O	R	E	■	G	E	A	R	■	A	C	E
L	O	I	N	■	E	A	S	E	■	S	E	W
E	N	S	I	G	N	■	E	A	T	S	■	■
■	■	M	U	D	■	S	C	R	I	P	T	■
M	O	B	■	T	A	P	■	H	O	N	O	R
A	D	O	S	■	S	E	A	■	D	E	L	I
N	O	R	M	A	■	T	W	O	■	T	O	M
E	R	R	O	R	S	■	A	N	T	■	■	■
■	■	O	G	R	E	■	K	E	E	P	E	R
D	E	W	■	I	D	L	E	■	M	O	R	E
A	Y	E	■	V	A	I	N	■	P	L	A	N
B	E	D	■	E	N	D	S	■	T	E	S	T

CROSSWORD 154

M	A	S	T	■	T	W	O	■	B	R	A	Y
E	C	H	O	■	H	I	M	■	R	A	T	E
S	H	O	E	T	R	E	E	■	O	P	E	N
H	E	W	■	H	O	L	L	O	W	■	■	■
■	■	M	E	N	D	E	D	■	S	A	T	■
A	W	N	I	N	G	■	T	E	M	P	L	E
C	H	I	N	■	■	■	■	O	A	T	S	■
R	E	C	I	P	E	■	C	A	N	N	O	T
E	Y	E	■	A	T	T	A	C	K	■	■	■
■	■	I	N	C	I	T	E	■	T	A	G	■
S	P	A	R	■	H	A	N	D	R	A	I	L
O	I	N	K	■	E	R	A	■	A	X	L	E
N	E	T	S	■	S	A	P	■	W	I	S	E

CROSSWORD 155

L	A	S	H	■	S	I	N	■	C	R	I	B
A	R	E	A	■	O	D	E	■	H	A	R	E
B	E	E	S	■	D	O	C	■	A	R	I	D
■	■	S	T	A	L	K	■	M	E	S	S	■
C	H	I	L	I	■	T	I	P	■	■	■	■
L	I	N	E	N	■	R	I	G	■	I	M	P
A	R	K	■	G	R	E	E	N	■	L	E	I
Y	E	S	■	L	I	D	■	O	W	L	E	T
■	■	R	E	V	■	R	I	S	K	Y	■	■
A	U	T	O	■	E	A	V	E	S	■	■	■
T	R	I	P	■	T	W	O	■	E	C	H	O
O	G	L	E	■	E	A	T	■	S	U	E	D
P	E	E	R	■	R	Y	E	■	T	E	N	D

CROSSWORD 156

T	E	L	L	■	G	R	I	P	■	G	O	B
O	R	A	L	■	L	A	C	E	■	A	D	E
M	A	M	A	■	E	M	E	R	A	L	D	S
■	■	M	E	N	■	■	C	A	S	T	■	■
B	L	E	A	T	■	G	N	A	T	■	■	■
R	I	O	■	C	R	O	I	S	S	A	N	T
I	N	N	■	H	A	U	N	T	■	L	E	I
M	E	S	S	E	N	G	E	R	■	S	O	N
■	■	U	R	G	E	■	A	M	O	N	G	■
O	G	R	E	■	■	B	Y	E	■	■	■	■
N	A	U	T	I	C	A	L	■	A	B	L	E
E	L	L	■	R	A	G	E	■	N	A	I	L
S	E	E	■	K	N	E	W	■	T	R	E	K

CROSSWORD 157

```
L A P   C H A R   T I C S
I R E   H E R E   O R A L
M E T   I R K S   W O R E
B A S I L     T A N N E D
    M I S H A P
W A S P   P O R E   P O P
E W E   B E A T S   A I R
D E W   A C R E   O N L Y
    R I D D E D
B A N A N A   A D O R E
A B E D   L E N T   P A Y
G L A D   T R E E   A G E
S E T S   Y A W N   L E D
```

CROSSWORD 158

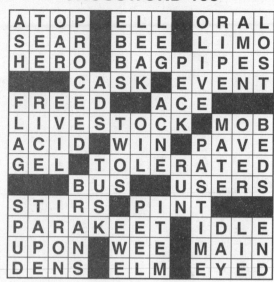

```
A T O P   E L L   O R A L
S E A R   B E E   L I M O
H E R O   B A G P I P E S
      C A S K   E V E N T
F R E E D   A C E
L I V E S T O C K   M O B
A C I D   W I N   P A V E
G E L   T O L E R A T E D
      B U S   U S E R S
S T I R S   P I N T
P A R A K E E T   I D L E
U P O N   W E E   M A I N
D E N S   E L M   E Y E D
```

CROSSWORD 159

```
P A S S   A W L   H I F I
I T C H   L E I   O V E N
C O A R S E S T   R Y E S
S P R E E   T E A R
      W A Y   R I O T E D
I C E D T E A   D R I V E
N O W   A N T   R E F
C L E A T   N U R S E R Y
H A S T E N   B A T
      T E A K   F O W L S
M A T E   M I S T R E A T
U P O N   E L L   M E N U
D E E D   S T Y   S P E D
```

CROSSWORD 160

```
G O A T   H U T   A B L E
O U C H   O N E   B L U E
T R E E   S I P   R O L L
      S P I T E   O W L S
S P H E R E   E R A
L E I   O R E   A D D E D
O A R   N Y L O N   A X E
T R E A T   F I G   R I M
      C O O   L E A N T O
S P O T   A M I S S
T A X I   S U E   K I T E
O P E N   I T S   E V E R
P A N G   S E T   D Y E R
```

CROSSWORD 161

```
Y A K   O B O E   S I T S
E W E   C R A M   A C H E
S L Y   C A F E   F E A T
    S T U D   R O A S T S
A C T O R   H A I R
S H O E   C E L L I S T S
P E N   S H A D Y   P E T
S W E L T E R S   F L E A
    E A S T   C U I N G
A L L E Y S   W A R N
L A I R   M O A N   T E A
A C N E   E D I T   E R R
S E E D   N E T S   R A T
```

CROSSWORD 162

```
B E D   S P E D   P A N S
A Y E   A L L Y   U N I T
R E N E G A D E   M E N U
      L A N E   C A W E D
R O A M   S P A
I N H E R I T E D   E L F
S C O R E R   W E E V I L
K E Y   C O A S T L I N E
      A N D   B L O W
S H A R P   M E M O
T A X I   F I R E W O O D
A L E S   O R A L   A I R
R O D E   R E S T   F L Y
```

CROSSWORD 163

```
P A D S   R O S E   A D S
O M I T   Y U L E   L A P
P E R I M E T E R   E R R
E N T R Y   P I G S T Y
      T A S T E R
W A R S H I P   R A B B I
E P I C   M O W   N E A T
D E B U T   R E A D E R S
    B E L T E D
S C R A P E   D O O R S
O L E   E A V E S D R O P
N U N   E V I L   D A L E
G E T   S E E K   S L E D
```

CROSSWORD 164

```
S O D   S C A R   S C A N
I R E   P O L O   P A C E
T E N D E R L Y   A R E A
    O D D   A R R E S T
L O F T   I S L E S
O N E   C A T   C E L L O
B Y E   L L A M A   A I D
E X T R A   R A P   I C E
    O I N K S   A R K S
S A L A M I   C A R
P R I M   P H A R M A C Y
A C R E   P O R T   S U E
S H E D   Y E A S   H E N
```

CROSSWORD 165

S	T	E	M		S	U	B	S		W	A	S
L	A	V	A		T	R	E	K		E	L	K
A	X	E	S		E	N	T	I	R	E	L	Y
P	I	N	K	I	E		S	P	A			
			S	P	R	Y			I	M	P	S
D	A	M		S	E	A		I	D	E	A	L
I	C	E		U	R	B	A	N		O	N	E
E	R	A	S	E		B	I	N		W	E	D
T	E	L	L		F	I	R	E				
		A	D	E		P	R	A	Y	E	R	
F	L	A	M	I	N	G	O		S	O	D	A
O	A	T		S	C	A	R		P	R	I	M
R	Y	E		K	E	P	T		S	E	T	S

CROSSWORD 166

S	A	P		S	L	A	W		T	A	G	S
P	I	E		H	I	R	E		A	C	R	E
A	L	P	H	A	B	E	T		T	H	I	N
			A	G	E				T	E	N	T
S	P	R	Y		L	A	D	L	E			
W	O	E	S			D	E	A	R	E	S	T
A	P	E		E	B	O	N	Y		V	O	W
M	E	D	D	L	E	R			M	E	M	O
			O	F	T	E	N		O	N	E	S
M	I	S	T			O	I	L				
E	D	I	T		P	R	O	C	E	E	D	S
T	O	R	E		E	A	S	E		L	O	P
S	L	E	D		A	W	E	D		K	E	Y

CROSSWORD 167

E	L	K		H	E	R		S	W	E	P	T
T	O	E		A	L	E		C	I	G	A	R
C	R	E	A	T	O	R		A	N	G	R	Y
H	E	L	D		P	A	W	N				
			A	R	E	N	A		S	N	A	P
G	A	P	P	E	D		D	E	L	U	X	E
A	C	U	T	E				Y	O	D	E	L
S	H	R	E	D	S		F	E	W	E	S	T
H	E	E	D		P	H	A	S	E			
			R	A	I	L		S	P	E	D	
M	A	I	N	E		P	L	A	T	E	A	U
A	C	T	E	D		P	E	W		A	S	K
T	E	S	T	S		O	N	E		T	E	E

CROSSWORD 168

A	C	R	E		C	A	N	E		A	S	H
W	H	E	N		O	X	E	N		P	I	E
L	I	E	S		L	E	A	T	H	E	R	S
S	P	L	I	C	E		T	E	E			
			G	A	S			R	A	G	E	S
D	W	I	N	D	L	E	D		L	A	V	A
R	I	D		A	Y	E			L	E	I	
A	L	L	Y		W	E	S	T	W	A	R	D
B	L	E	E	D			P	A	R			
			A	R	C		I	R	I	S	E	S
C	H	A	R	I	O	T	S		T	A	X	I
O	A	R		F	R	E	E		E	M	I	T
G	Y	M		T	E	N	D		S	E	T	S

383